SERENA WILLIAMS

SERENA WILLIAMS

MATT CHRISTOPHER®

The #1 Sports Series for Kids

with Stephanie True Peters

LITTLE, BROWN AND COMPANY
New York   Boston

Little, Brown and Company
Hachette Book Group
1290 Avenue of the Americas, New York, NY 10104
Visit us at lb-kids.com
mattchristopher.com

Text adapted from *On the Court with... Venus and Serena Williams*,
published in May 2002 by Little, Brown and Company
First Edition: July 2017

Little, Brown and Company is a division of Hachette Book Group, Inc.
The Little, Brown name and logo are trademarks of Hachette Book Group, Inc.

The publisher is not responsible for websites (or their content)
that are not owned by the publisher.

Matt Christopher® is a registered trademark of Matt Christopher Royalties, Inc.

Text written by Stephanie True Peters

Library of Congress Cataloging-in-Publication Data
Names: Peters, Stephanie True, 1968– author.
Title: Serena Williams / With Stephanie True Peters.
Description: First edition. | New York : Little, Brown Books for Young Readers, 2017. | Series:
Legends in sports | "By Matt Christopher® The #1 Sports Series for Kids." | Audience: Age 8–12.
Identifiers: LCCN 2017009568 | ISBN 9780316471800 (paperback) | ISBN 9780316471831
(ebook) | ISBN 9780316471824 (library edition ebook)
Subjects: LCSH: Williams, Serena, 1981—Juvenile literature. | African American women tennis
players—Biography—Juvenile literature. | Tennis players—United States—Biography—Juvenile
literature. | BISAC: JUVENILE NONFICTION / Biography & Autobiography / Sports &
Recreation. | JUVENILE NONFICTION / Biography & Autobiography / Women. | JUVENILE
NONFICTION / Sports & Recreation / Racket Sports. | JUVENILE NONFICTION / Sports &
Recreation / Olympics. | JUVENILE NONFICTION / Sports & Recreation / General. |
JUVENILE NONFICTION / Biography & Autobiography / Cultural Heritage.
Classification: LCC GV994.W55 P48 2017 | DDC 796.342092 [B]—dc23
LC record available at https://lccn.loc.gov/2017009568

ISBNs: 978-0-316-47180-0 (pbk.), 978-0-316-47183-1 (ebook)

Printed in the United States of America

LSC-C

10 9 8 7 6 5 4 3 2 1

Contents

★ CHAPTER ONE ★
1984

Just Swing

Six o'clock one warm summer morning in 1984, Richard Williams and his wife, Oracene Price, loaded their yellow Volkswagen minibus with a shopping cart and several milk crates full of tennis balls. They added tennis rackets and a broom. Then they called for their five daughters—Yetunde, Isha, Lyndrea, Venus, and Serena. The girls clambered into the van. One of the older ones helped Serena, who was not quite four, into her seat.

The family drove from their modest home in Compton, California, to a nearby public park. Richard pulled into a small lot adjacent to the tennis courts. No one was playing tennis on them, though a few young men lingered on the sidelines, just hanging out. Glass from broken bottles and fast-food wrappers littered the playing area. Graffiti was spray-painted on the surface.

1

Undeterred, Richard and Oracene ushered their daughters from the van and retrieved the balls, broom, and rackets. While the three older girls helped sweep up, Serena got into her stroller, and Venus pushed her to one side of the court.

When the surfaces were clear of debris, the four older girls grabbed rackets and hurried onto the courts with their mother. Serena stayed in her stroller. It's what she usually did during these outings.

But not this time. This time, her father held out a racket and motioned for her to join him.

She got out of the stroller and took the racket. It was almost as big as she was and felt heavy in her small hands. She was too excited to notice. After watching her sisters from the sidelines for as long as she could remember, she was finally getting her turn to play.

Her father tossed a tennis ball in the air and hit it gently over the net to her. "Swing at the ball," he called out.

She giggled and swung. Her momentum spun her almost completely around. Her white tennis skirt with purple, pink, and gray flowers flared out in a bell. She missed the ball, which bounced and rolled away.

"Just swing," her father instructed.

For the next hour they stood in the hot sun, father and daughter, as Williams patiently taught his youngest how to strike a tennis ball with a tennis racket. At first she hit the ball mostly by accident. Richard occasionally stopped, placed his hand around his daughter's on the racket, and showed her how to sweep it through the air and hit the ball in the center of the racket's strings. She began to make consistent contact.

When the crates were empty, they gathered up the loose balls, making a game of seeing who could get the most, and started over. Finally, Richard held up a ball. "Last one!" he called out.

"Last one," Serena responded with a laugh. He tapped the ball toward her, and she swung.

Thwack! The ball made a distinctive sound as it struck the racket's strings. Oracene and the other girls cheered. Then they gathered up the equipment, loaded it back into the van, and returned home.

For the four older girls, that early morning tennis practice was like most other morning practices. For the youngest, however, it was the first step toward the making of a champion.

A champion named Serena Williams.

★ CHAPTER TWO ★

THE PAST

Before Serena

The story of Serena Williams begins in an unlikely place: Compton, California. Then as now, Compton was poor, and many residents of the mostly African American and Hispanic inner-city community struggled to make ends meet. The buildings were run-down. Crime and poverty were rampant. Gang members sold drugs and engaged in other illegal activities in public places—including the parks where Richard took the girls to play tennis.

Sometimes, the gang members told Richard that he and his girls weren't welcome. Williams refused to be intimidated. He stood up for his right to use the courts. Eventually, the locals left them in peace.

But the parks were still dangerous places to be.

One afternoon when Serena was about seven, she was with her father and Venus at East Compton Park (now East Rancho Dominguez Park). Midway through practice, a carload of young men cruised by the courts. One of the men stuck a gun out the window and started shooting.

"At first, I just thought someone was setting off firecrackers or popping some balloons," Serena said years later.

Venus, Serena, and Richard hit the ground as bullets flew all around them. Gang members hanging out in the park ran and hid. Seconds later, the firing stopped and the car sped away.

Serena and Venus were shaken up by the drive-by shooting, but Richard calmed them down. Keeping a watchful eye out, he convinced them to resume practice.

"There was no place in the world that was rougher than Compton," Richard once commented. "The ghetto will make you rough, it'll make you tough, it'll make you strong."

Richard wanted his girls to grow up strong. He also wanted them to have a future beyond Compton. Their future was all he and Oracene were thinking about when they decided to teach their daughters to play tennis. And not just play—the goal was for them to become world-class professional players.

According to Williams family lore, Richard came

up with that goal long before Serena was born. He was a recreational tennis player himself, and he'd taught Oracene to play. When he heard that a professional player named Virginia Ruzici had earned more than $30,000 for winning a major tennis event, he decided that was what his children should do. He told Oracene his idea to develop the girls into professional players. She agreed it was worth pursuing. Inspired and determined, Richard drew up a seventy-eight-page plan for achieving their goal. If that plan was successful, their girls would never experience want.

Richard knew all about want. He'd grown up in Shreveport, Louisiana, in the 1940s amid abject poverty and racism. His father abandoned the family when Richard was young, leaving his mother, Julia Mae, to raise six children on her own.

Richard did whatever he could to help his mother and sisters survive. He hunted and fished for food. He set up a farm stand and grew fruits and vegetables to sell. Sometimes, if he didn't have enough produce to stock the stand, he stole what he needed from other people's gardens.

When he was older, Richard left Louisiana to make his way in the world. He met Oracene in Michigan in 1979. She and Richard married soon afterward. A widow, Oracene was raising seven-year-old Yetunde, six-year-old Isha, and one-year-old Lyndrea on her own. Oracene gave birth to Venus Ebony Starr Williams on June 17, 1980, and Serena Jameka Williams on September 26, 1981.

The family of seven settled in Compton, where Oracene worked as a nurse and Richard ran a small security company. In his spare time, Richard learned everything he could about tennis. He read books about the game. He watched matches on television and studied videos about the sport. He played with and against more experienced players, honing his skills and fine-tuning his techniques.

Most important, he played tennis with his daughters. At first, it was just the three oldest, Yetunde, Isha, and Lyndrea. "Life was get up, six o'clock in the morning, go to the tennis court before school," Isha once told a reporter. "After school, go to tennis." They were good players; in fact, some say Isha might have turned professional if not for back problems.

But right from the start, Venus and Serena brought something special to the court. Maybe it was because they'd started playing when they were very young. Or maybe they just had a natural athletic ability perfectly suited for tennis. Whatever the case, Richard believed that "something special" would one day propel them into the upper stratosphere of tennis. If so, they would join a very small list of successful African American players.

The first great African American tennis player was a woman named Ora Mae Washington. She played in tournaments run by the American Tennis Association (ATA), a group formed in 1916 after the United States Lawn Tennis Association (USLTA—later the USTA, when the word *Lawn* was dropped) refused to allow African Americans to take part in their competitions. From 1929 to 1937, Washington won eight ATA singles titles and twelve doubles titles. That stretch of victories earned her the nickname "the Queen of Tennis."

Then came Althea Gibson. Like Washington, Gibson was limited to the ATA tournaments, where she crushed her opponents throughout the 1940s and early 1950s. The USLTA took notice, and in 1950, they reversed their rule and invited her to play in their premier event, the US Open. She accepted and so became the first African American, male *or* female, to play in that tournament. She lost in an early round, but her supporters didn't care. She'd broken the professional tennis color barrier, a remarkable achievement by anyone's standards.

And she was just getting warmed up.

The US Open is one of four tournaments known collectively as the Grand Slam. The other three are the Australian Open, the French Open, and Wimbledon. Winning one Grand Slam tournament in a career is a significant accomplishment. More than one? Not something that happens very often—unless the player is a truly superb athlete and fierce competitor.

Althea Gibson was both. From 1956 to 1958, she dominated in all three tennis events: singles, where one player faces another; doubles, where a pair of players of the same gender competes against another pair of that same gender; and mixed doubles, where male and female partners play against another male-female partnership. Gibson won the women's singles title at the 1956 French Open, and at Wimbledon and the US Open in 1957 and 1958. She also chalked up victories in doubles and mixed doubles at the same Grand Slam tournaments in 1956, 1957, and 1958.

Gibson was ranked first among female tennis players in the world when she retired in 1958. *Time* and *Sports Illustrated* magazines both featured her on their covers that year, the first black woman ever to be pictured on either. The *Associated Press* named her Female Athlete of the Year.

Gibson left an indelible mark on the sport. So did Arthur Ashe. Using a quick and decisive serve-and-volley style of play—a technique where the player serves the ball and immediately rushes the net to attack the serve return—he won the men's singles tournament at the US Open in 1968, the first African American man to do so. He added the Australian Open title in 1970 and Wimbledon in 1975—two more firsts.

Yet despite such strong role models, very few African Americans took up the sport in those decades. Richard Williams was an exception. He turned himself into a player and then a coach. He worked with his two youngest girls on their forehands, backhands, serves, and volleys for several hours each week. They stretched, conditioned, and ran. They played with, and against, each other and some of their father's friends.

Their hard work paid off. Their hits grew more powerful. Their reaction time quickened. Their instincts sharpened and their shots became more precise. They were so good that a few short years after Serena first held a racket, Richard and Oracene decided it was time for them to move beyond the Compton public courts and into a more competitive arena: the USTA.

★ CHAPTER THREE ★

1985–1989

Ten-and-Under

The plan for introducing Serena and Venus to USTA play was simple. Venus, who was older, more athletic, and stronger, would compete in the Southern California ten-and-under junior tournaments. Eight-year-old Serena, meanwhile, would hone her skills in a less challenging recreational league. They'd both improve by playing against unknown competition, but because they'd be in different leagues, they wouldn't face each other across the net — something Richard and Oracene wanted to avoid.

Eight-year-old Serena understood the plan, but she didn't like it. She knew she wasn't as good as Venus, but after watching a few of her sister's matches, she believed she was as good or better than the girls Venus was playing. Week after week, she asked her father to let her enter the ten-and-under tournaments, too. Week after week, he refused.

So Serena took matters into her own hands.

Venus was scheduled to play in a junior tournament at Indian Wells, California. Unbeknownst to her father, Serena got a copy of the tournament application form, filled it out, and entered herself.

"I didn't say anything to anybody," Serena later recalled. "Not even my sisters."

All eyes were on Venus the day of the tournament. That made it easy for Serena to sneak off to face her own competition. She was midway through her first match before Richard discovered she was playing. It was too late to pull her off the court, so he settled in to watch.

What he saw impressed him.

Many young tennis players struggle to get the ball over the net on a consistent basis. They make unforced errors, meaning they send the ball out-of-bounds or into the net. More experienced players can earn points with forced errors, which come by purposefully making a shot that is difficult to return.

The youngest player in the tournament, Serena could already hit the ball powerfully and accurately with forehand or two-handed backhand shots. She had a powerful serve for her age. Most importantly, she had a keen understanding of tennis strategy.

"The concept of hitting it where your opponent isn't, of playing to win...somehow those things were instinctive with me," Serena recalled. "I knew to put the ball away for a winner."

Serena beat her first opponent by forcing her to run for every shot. She was thrilled—until she saw Richard.

Her father was not one to take kindly to disobedience. "I was prepared for punishment," she admitted later.

She needn't have worried. Richard was the first to congratulate her after her victory. He even joked with her about having to pay her forty-dollar entry fee.

Venus won her first match, too. And her second, and the others that followed. So did Serena. They eliminated players one by one until they were the only two left!

The situation Richard and Oracene had most wanted to avoid was about to happen: their girls were going to face each other in the finals. Mom and Dad were nervous wrecks watching Serena and Venus warm up.

Serena wasn't nervous, though. That day, she'd discovered she could beat older, more experienced players. She'd proved to her father and to herself that she could hold her own in the ten-and-under junior tournaments. She suspected she'd lose in the finals — an accurate prediction, for Venus won the best-of-three-sets match easily with scores of 6–2, 6–2 — but she didn't mind. Venus was her sister. She wanted the best for her and knew Venus felt the same about her. All things considered, losing to Venus was no big deal.

Until she saw her sister's shiny gold trophy.

As runner-up, Serena had won a silver trophy. But she wanted the gold — badly.

Venus took one look at Serena's face and knew exactly what her sister was feeling. She could have teased Serena with her golden award. Instead, she demonstrated just what a caring person she was by insisting she preferred silver to gold and asking Serena to trade trophies with her.

Venus's generous gesture must have reassured Richard and Oracene that they didn't have to worry about the girls competing against each other because they allowed Serena to join the ten-and-under league. But there were still other challenges ahead in the junior tennis circuit.

Most of the other girls in their Southern California league had learned tennis in private clubs. Many had already received professional instruction. They knew one another from private clinics and tennis camps. There were few African American players, and fewer still who had learned the game from a parent.

In short, people weren't quite sure what to make of the Williams sisters. Some marveled that their unconventional training had produced such strong players. They applauded their abilities. But others treated the Williams girls poorly, ignoring them or acting as if they didn't belong. Often, these people were tennis parents who took the tournaments far too seriously. They were pushy with their children, yelled at their kids after a loss, and argued with tournament officials.

The worst of the lot muttered racial comments about them. Part of the reason was simple jealousy — the girls were winning.

But Richard and Oracene recognized that some people at the tournaments were flat-out prejudiced. They did what they could to prepare their daughters for verbal attacks, encouraging them not to let the hurtful words get to them on the court and to channel their feelings into their play. Eight-year-old Serena and nine-year-old Venus did their best to follow this guidance — and they still do today.

"Be strong. Be black.... Play angry, but let them

see confidence," Serena wrote in a special "match book" she keeps with her during tournaments.

In the end, the girls let their records speak for them. Venus moved up to the twelve-and-under league, where she went undefeated with sixty-three wins, no losses. Serena, meanwhile, stayed in the ten-and-under bracket, finishing with a record of 46–3. Both were ranked number one in their leagues and were poised to power through the Southern California junior tennis circuit in the coming years.

But Richard and Oracene had other plans — plans that took them and their daughters to a new home and a new way of life.

✷ CHAPTER FOUR ✷

1990–1991

Good-bye, Compton; Hello, Florida

Unlike some professional sports, tennis cultivates players at a very young age, sometimes as young as ten. Coaches keep careful watch on activity in the junior leagues to see whose names are at the top. By 1990, that name was Venus Williams. Her fast-paced, aggressive play impressed fans, coaches, and even a handful of professional players, who were amazed to see such strength in someone so young.

Serena may not have been quite as powerful then, but she still had fans.

"Everybody was talking about Venus," recalled tennis great Zina Garrison, an African American player who'd made a big splash in the late '80s and early '90s. "But, for me, it was the little one that struck me. She was poaching at the net, fist-bumping and just having a ball. You could see they were both very talented, but in my mind I kind of always believed Serena was going to be the best."

Still, Venus was the main attraction. People whispered that she'd turn pro when she was fourteen, the age of eligibility. That was still a few years off, and yet the Williamses knew it was time to start preparing for that possibility. First, though, they needed to make some bigger changes.

Venus's notoriety was making it difficult to remain in Compton. People thought they were wealthy, and Richard and Oracene worried that their family would be at risk if they remained there. The underlying racial tension in the junior circuit was also a concern, as was the ongoing gang violence in their neighborhood.

Then there was the coaching. Richard and Oracene had done an amazing job with the girls, but they'd taken them about as far as they could. If Venus and Serena were to improve, they needed someone who could help them reach the next level and beyond. Florida had the best training facilities, so Richard and Oracene reached out to several coaches there.

One of those coaches was Rick Macci of the International Tennis Academy at Grenelefe. Macci had trained young tennis phenom Jennifer Capriati, who had reached the semifinals in both Wimbledon and the US Open that year at the tender age of fifteen. Macci hoped Venus would be just as successful under his tutelage.

Macci flew to California to watch Venus play. He liked what he saw and at one point commented that Richard had the next Michael Jordan on his hands. Richard immediately responded that he had *two* Michael Jordans. Venus was one. Serena was the other. Richard knew Venus had the makings of an outstanding player, but he believed just as much in Serena—and he made sure Macci paid attention to her, too.

Macci and his academy seemed like a good fit for the Williams girls, so Richard and Oracene committed to the move. They also committed to something else: a decision to pull Venus and Serena off the junior tennis circuit.

The decision was wildly controversial in the tennis world. Some observers charged that Richard Williams was sabotaging his daughters' careers. The top junior tournaments were where they would test their abilities and improve their play, after all. Professional players also voiced their opinions. "I don't agree with the path the Williamses have taken with their career," said legendary superstar Chris Evert. "I still advise kids to play the juniors."

Richard and Oracene didn't see it that way. Young players on the junior circuit often have to travel to tournaments. Tournaments last a few days, sometimes longer, and happen all year long. The Williamses didn't want to subject their daughters to that kind of schedule — or to the racism they believed they would meet at some tournaments. They wanted Venus and Serena to have time to focus on their education, too, in case their careers as professional tennis players didn't work out. And, as Richard told Serena later, "Meeka, there wasn't any point in traveling all around the country to watch you and V beat up on all those little girls."

While Macci might not have agreed with the decision, he didn't pressure the Williamses to change their minds. Venus and Serena were his students, but they were Richard and Oracene's children.

Having settled on Macci's tennis school, the family said good-bye to Compton in the summer of 1991. Only Yetunde, who was starting college, stayed behind. The rest piled into a Winnebago and headed for Haines City, Florida, to begin the next chapter in their lives.

★ CHAPTER FIVE ★

1991–1993

Growing Up on the Court

The Williamses' new life in Florida began almost immediately, and Serena soon wished she was back in California.

"I didn't like my new school," she wrote years later. "I thought it was only a matter of time before these kids started picking on me."

Tennis was different, too. In California, her father had made conditioning, stretching, and running fun. Not so at the academy, where workouts felt like *work*.

Macci trained his students hard for a reason. A tennis match can last for hours, so a player must develop stamina. To win, she must do more than simply hit the ball over the net. She must hit it with power and control. She must be fast on her feet so she can get to every ball.

She also must become a student of the game. She has to learn to read her opponent and anticipate where the next shot is likely to go. She has to understand when to put spin on the ball and how a ball with spin is going to move. (Topspin rotates the ball toward the opponent. When the ball hits the court, it skims low like a stone skipping across water. Backspin balls rotate away from the opponent and bounce backward. Players who can't recognize spin often end up lunging awkwardly for the ball or missing it completely.) She has to learn when to charge the net and hit volleys, which are shots struck before the ball has hit the ground, and when to stay back and hit ground strokes — shots hit after the ball has bounced — from the baseline. She has to figure out how to force her opponent out of position and then follow up with a winning, unreturnable shot. And she has to be prepared to chase after those same shots herself.

Speed, agility, quick reflexes, and knowledge of the game — that's what Macci was teaching the Williams sisters. They already had the focus, determination, and desire to win. They were great players but needed to become champions. "They would run over broken glass to get a ball," Macci once told a reporter.

Richard and Oracene appreciated Macci's approach, but they were also mindful of the possibility that the rigorous training regimen could backfire. If the girls started to resent the drills or tire of the constant demand put on their young bodies, they might lose their desire to play. Or they might buckle under the pressure to improve and to win, and burn out before their careers even began.

The Williamses were determined not to let that happen to their daughters. That's why the entire family moved to Florida. Plenty of tennis students live at their academies. But the Williamses stayed together to give Venus and Serena the emotional support they needed to succeed.

The girls remained under Macci's tutelage for two years. By most accounts, their play improved and their enthusiasm for the game never dwindled. Yet Richard wasn't satisfied. He and Macci had clashed in the past, particularly over the decision to keep the girls off the junior tournament circuit. As time went on, their relationship deteriorated.

One reason for this may have been Richard's insistence on being involved in his daughters' training. The academy teachers were accustomed to parents who simply turned their children over to them and let them control every aspect of their game.

Richard Williams was not that kind of parent. He and Oracene had gotten Venus and Serena to where they were, which was far ahead of many girls their age. He had no intention of being shut out. Although he never really stated why, a few years after their move from Compton, he removed Venus and Serena from Macci's academy.

The family moved to Pompano Beach, Florida, and began to train with another famous coach, Nick Bollettieri. They didn't stay with him long, either. In the end, Richard stepped back in and resumed his role as the girls' primary coach.

Not long after the move, Richard and Oracene made another change. They pulled the girls out of the middle school when Serena was midway through seventh grade and Venus eighth grade, and began homeschooling them instead.

At first, the move and changes to her schooling and tennis schedules didn't bother Serena. But after a short while, she began to feel lost. "I'd always loved the classroom part," she wrote. "It was all that stuff that went on in the hallways and the cafeteria that gave me trouble."

Then there was the tennis. At Grenelefe, she'd been challenged by the drills, lessons, and level of play. She didn't always like training there, but at least she knew at the end of the day, she'd leave the academy behind and go home. But at Pompano Beach, the courts were so near to their house that she often felt as though she couldn't escape them.

"They were always calling to me, and calling to me, only not in a good way," she remembered of those nearby courts.

Serena's interest in the sport dwindled. Her motivation to improve stalled. She was bored with the routine of morning tennis, at-home lessons, and then more tennis in the afternoon—and boredom never breeds champions.

In short, Serena needed a push to keep moving forward. And in 1994, she got it.

★ CHAPTER SIX ★

1994–1995

Pro or No?

In 1994, the Women's Tennis Association (WTA) came under a great deal of criticism when Jennifer Capriati, one-time tennis prodigy and Macci's former student, crashed and burned. She had played in her first tournament just before she turned fourteen and enjoyed several years of spectacular success. Then the pressure got to her. She abandoned the game and at age eighteen ended up in drug rehabilitation. Many observers blamed the WTA for allowing her to become a professional at such a young age, before she was emotionally and physically mature enough to handle it.

The WTA responded by changing the rules. Originally, a player could turn pro around the age of fourteen. In late 1994, they changed that age to sixteen and also ruled that players under eighteen would only be allowed to participate in a limited number of tournaments. But there was a loophole: fourteen-year-olds who turned professional *before* the end of 1994 would be able to compete in professional events under the old rules, with no restrictions on the number of events they could play.

Venus had turned fourteen years old on June 17, 1994. She'd developed into an astonishingly strong player. She hadn't played in a tournament since leaving Compton three and a half years earlier but was more than ready to test herself against her peers. So after much discussion within the family, Richard and Oracene decided to let her turn pro.

The decision came as a huge surprise to many in the tennis world. After all, Richard had been very outspoken about his refusal to let Venus and Serena play in junior tournaments. He'd been just as candid with his opinion about players who turned pro at such a young age. "Kids who turn pro at fourteen, I really don't believe it's the kids' idea, it's the parents' idea," Richard Williams commented to a reporter in 1993. "If I encouraged Venus to turn pro now, that would be wrong."

But according to Serena, when the rule changed, Venus pressured Richard and Oracene to let her go pro right away. "Venus can be pretty forceful when she sets her mind to something," she wrote. "Daddy had no choice but to cave."

Venus made her professional debut that November at the Bank of the West Classic in California. It was a relatively minor event in the tennis world. But Venus's presence made a major impact. Even though she hadn't played in the junior circuit, people knew about her. They showed up to see the phenom from Florida.

Serena couldn't have been happier for her sister. And she had time on the court at the tournament, too, as Venus's warm-up partner. She cheered the loudest on the sidelines when Venus won her first match. But those cheers grew even more robust at the start of her second match, when Venus took the first set, 6–2, from the tournament's top-seeded player, Arantxa Sánchez-Vicario, and went up in the second set 3–1.

Those three games were the last Venus won in that tournament, however. Sánchez-Vicario powered back to win the set 6–3, then took the final set 6–0.

Venus played three tournaments in 1995, losing in the first round in the first two and reaching the quarterfinals in the third before being beaten. Serena was in the stands for all three. It wasn't where she wanted to be, though. More than anything, she wanted to be on the court. She believed she could be just as competitive as Venus if she was given the chance. Two things stood in the way: her father and the WTA's age eligibility rule.

Overcoming the first obstacle was relatively easy. Like Venus, Serena kept at Richard until she persuaded him to let her play. When reporters questioned why he reversed himself—again—Williams had a reply many parents could appreciate.

"You can't really say no to these kids these days, not the way parents did in my day. And to be honest, if I did, I'm afraid I'd lose them," he said.

As for the age eligibility rule, if Serena played in one professional tournament before the end of 1995, she'd be cleared to continue as a professional and not have to wait two years until she was sixteen. So just a month after her fourteenth birthday, Serena turned pro by playing in her first tournament, the Bell Classic in Quebec.

It was hardly a classic for Serena, though. She misfired shots. Her timing was off. She was chasing balls rather than making her opponent, a relatively unknown player named Annie Miller, run around. With every unforced error, her self-confidence ebbed. She lost in straight sets, 1–6, 1–6, in less than an hour.

"I felt bad out there because I lost," she told a sportswriter afterward. "I didn't play like I meant to play. I played kind of like an amateur."

Serena kept a low profile after the Bell Classic,

staying out of tournaments for seventeen months. She didn't stay away from the courts, however. The boredom she'd felt just a year earlier had vanished. In its place was 100 percent motivation — to fix what wasn't working and perfect what was, to show up at her next pro outing stronger, faster, and more confident, and to fight her way past the competition and to the top.

★ CHAPTER SEVEN ★

1996

Entering the Spotlight

Women's tennis, like most sports, surges in popularity when it has superstars—athletes who dominate the sport and bring a certain charisma to it. The sport had its stars through the '60s, '70s, and '80s with Billie Jean King, Martina Navratilova, and Chris Evert. In the late 1980s and early 1990s, a new generation of women's tennis stars seemed ready to take over and build on the accomplishments of their predecessors.

But many of these prospects didn't last long. Tracy Austin and Jennifer Capriati burned out. Emerging champion Monica Seles was injured when she was attacked by a mentally ill fan. While there were still many outstanding players, Steffi Graf in particular, none had that special extra spark that drew new fans to the sport. To grow in popularity, tennis needed a new generation of players to take over.

Many predicted that Venus would be the next big star in women's tennis, and that Serena wasn't far behind. Their "straight outta Compton" background story captivated the sports world, for it showed that anyone could make it in tennis and that you didn't have to be wealthy to play. African Americans who had paid little attention to the sport before began to track their progress. Even people who weren't tennis fans were intrigued by them.

Those anticipating that the Williams sisters were going to take the tennis scene by storm after their debuts were in for a disappointment. The girls returned to Florida and resumed their usual routine of school— no longer homeschooled, they were attending a local high school then—and hours of daily tennis practice.

But it wasn't all tennis. They were now teenagers, and they liked to do the same things most girls their age do. Both loved music and kept up with all the popular bands. They spent a lot of free time with their pet dogs and looked forward to learning how to drive when they turned sixteen. Because tennis is an international sport, Venus and Serena studied Italian and French. They'd later surprise some members of the foreign press by responding to questions in both languages.

And they were dedicated to their Christian faith. Oracene raised them and their sisters as Jehovah's Witnesses, members of a religious order with deep-felt devotion to God and the teachings of Jesus and the Bible. Serena and Venus still belong to this order today and often credit their faith for giving them inner strength and stability.

Venus took time out of the routine in 1996 to play in five events. She made it to the third round in one, but didn't last beyond the first round in the other four. In 1997, the number of tournaments she entered jumped to fifteen.

Among those was her first appearance at Wimbledon, the prestigious English tournament based at the All England Lawn Tennis and Croquet Club and the only Grand Slam tournament played on grass courts. Venus had long dreamed about playing there and had once told Richard that Wimbledon was the one tournament she really wanted to win. Playing against Magdalena Grzybowska, she rolled to a 6–4 win in the first set and staked out a 2–0 lead in the second. Then she suddenly fell apart. Grzybowska's backhand mystified Venus, who lost, 6–4, 2–6, 4–6. She was disappointed but philosophical, saying, "It's my first Wimbledon and there will be many more."

Venus rebounded at the US Open in September, battling her way into the finals to face Martina Hingis. Like Venus, Hingis was a seventeen-year-old phenom who had started playing at a very young age. But unlike Venus, Hingis had played in junior tournaments before turning pro. That experience may have given her an edge, for she hammered Venus in the finals, 6–0, 6–4.

Two months later, it was Serena's turn. That November, she entered the Ameritech Cup in Chicago. It was only her fifth professional tournament, yet the sixteen-year-old picked apart her opponents, working her way up the ladder toward the final rounds.

One of those opponents was the fifth-ranked player in the world, Mary Pierce. Pierce was six years older than Serena, a veteran of tournaments and a highly skilled player. But as talented and experienced as she was, she couldn't beat Serena. With the crowd cheering her every point, the unranked rookie took the first set 6–3 and then outplayed Pierce in a tiebreaker to win the second set 7–6.

"I think I discouraged her when I chased down and got back some of her best shots," a delighted Serena said after the match. "A lot of players would not get them at all."

That win set up a quarterfinal meeting with another hugely talented player, Monica Seles. After Serena's performance against Pierce, fans were expecting a good match.

They were not disappointed — unless they were rooting for Seles. After dropping the first set 4–6, Serena dug deep and delivered what one newspaper called "an awesome display of power." She burned Seles in the second set 6–1, winning the last point with an ace. Showing no signs of slowing, she roared to a 5–1 lead in the third and deciding set. She was one point away from victory when Seles knocked over a little drop shot — a soft shot that falls just over the net. Such shots are often winners, unreturnable because the opposing player can't reach them in time.

Serena reached it. With a powerful, lightning-fast swing of her racket, she fired it past Seles for the win. Serena was in the semifinals!

Sadly for her growing number of fans, that was as far as she got. Lindsay Davenport, an accomplished player with much more tournament experience under her belt, defeated Serena in straight sets with identical scores of 6–4, 6–4.

Serena's hopes of reaching the finals were over, but she wasn't too disappointed. For years, sportswriters and tennis enthusiasts had praised one Williams sister—Venus. Serena had always celebrated her big sister's accomplishments. Yet she had felt overshadowed by them, too.

Now, at long last, she was getting her moment in the spotlight.

★ CHAPTER EIGHT ★
1997–1998

Williams vs. Williams

The world of sports loves great rivalries, and tennis is no exception. Favorite past matchups include superstars Ivan Lendl versus John McEnroe, Martina Navratilova versus Chris Evert, Steffi Graf versus Monica Seles, and Roger Federer versus Novak Djokovic. In the late 1990s, though, one head-to-head competition was on everyone's must-watch list: Venus Williams versus Serena Williams.

Everyone's, that is, except the Williams family. From the very beginning, Richard and Oracene had worked to keep the sisters' tournament schedules separate. But as 1997 wound down, they realized that was no longer possible. The girls were simply too good. They were both slated to play in most of the major and minor tennis events. An on-court meeting in 1998 seemed inevitable.

It came at one of the first and biggest tennis

tournaments of the year—the Australian Open. Held in Melbourne at the end of January, the Australian Open kicks off the Grand Slam schedule; the French Open comes next, in late May to early June, with Wimbledon a month later, followed by the US Open in early September.

In tournament play, players are matched up, or seeded, in brackets according to their ranks in the tennis world. The two highest-ranked players are in separate brackets. They play each other only if they make it to the finals. Unseeded players are distributed throughout the tournament according to a draw.

When the Australian Open schedule was released, Venus and Serena discovered that if they both won their first-round matches, they'd have to play each other in the second round!

It was sixteen-year-old Serena's first Grand Slam event, and winning that preliminary round was no guarantee. Yet she entered it feeling confident. Earlier that month, she had stunned spectators by dispatching Lindsay Davenport in the quarterfinals of the Medibank International in Sydney, Australia.

The first player Serena faced in her Grand Slam debut was Irina Spîrlea. Spîrlea had a checkered history with the Williams family. The year before, she was losing to Venus in the semifinals of the US Open. During a change of sides, she strode purposefully toward the sidelines, whistling in a carefree manner. Venus was moving the same way, apparently intent on reaching her chair. Spîrlea, on the other hand, was intent on reaching Venus. She ran into her, jabbing her knee into the side of Venus's knee.

"It looks as though she deliberately collided with her opponent, Venus Williams," a surprised announcer reported shortly after the incident.

Venus shrugged it off and went on to defeat Spîrlea.

Now it was Serena's turn to beat Spîrlea. And she did just that, winning the third and final set when Irina hit the ball into the net. Serena was joyful afterward, raising her arms and grinning broadly. She was gracious, too, telling reporters that she held no grudge against Spîrlea for what she had done to Venus. Still, Serena delivered a subtle jab of her own, noting how tough it must have been for Spîrlea, the sixth-seeded player in the tournament, to lose to the fifty-third seed in the first round.

Later that day, Venus defeated her opponent, Alexia Dechaume-Balleret, 6–3, 6–0, setting up the match the tennis world had been waiting for: Williams versus Williams. Although Serena had practiced against

Venus countless times and played her in juniors, playing her sister in a professional tournament—and a Grand Slam at that—was another matter entirely. She wanted to win every time she stepped on the court, but she wanted Venus to win, too. And truth be told, she believed Venus *would* win.

"I didn't think I'd have a shot," she admitted.

The crowd at center court for the second-round matchup was uncharacteristically quiet, as if the spectators sensed the girls were uncomfortable with the situation.

Venus and Serena were tense, and it showed in their play. Each made a number of unforced errors in the first set. For a while, it seemed as if neither sister really wanted to win.

With the set tied at 6–6, Venus finally got an edge. After a long rally, Serena sent a forehand wide. Venus took advantage and won a tiebreaker, 7–4, to take the set, 7–6.

The defeat seemed to make Serena lose confidence. She kept double-faulting, which is when a player hits both serves out-of-bounds. Venus won the second set, 6–1, to take the match.

But Venus didn't celebrate after her victory. She met Serena at the net and gave her a hug, and then the two sisters held hands and bowed to the crowd. As they walked off the court, still holding hands, Venus said softly to Serena, "I'm sorry I took you out. I didn't want to, but I had to do it."

Serena took the loss in stride. "If I had to lose in the second round, there's no one better to lose to than Venus." When a reporter asked Venus, who would fall to Lindsay Davenport in the quarterfinals, if the match was fun, Venus sighed and said, "Was it fun? . . . I think it would have been great fun if it was the final. . . . Serena hates to lose, and her reputation is that she doesn't lose to anyone twice. So I'm going to be practicing secretly if I want to win the next one."

As it turned out, there were plenty of "next ones" in their future.

⋆ CHAPTER NINE ⋆
1998

Rising Stars

The Williams sisters' rivalry and powerful play sparked a popular revival of women's tennis. They were part of a new generation of female players who captured the imagination of fans. Competition had never been tougher, as a half dozen or more players in each tournament had a good chance to win every time they played. Top-ranked Martina Hingis was the most accomplished player in the game, followed by other young stars, such as Lindsay Davenport, Mary Pierce, and Anna Kournikova, and veterans Steffi Graf and Monica Seles. Women's tennis had rarely been so competitive. There was more interest in the sport than there had been in years.

But the sisters' rise to the top was not without its rough spots. In the 1998 French Open, Serena made it into the fourth round and then had to face Arantxa

Sánchez-Vicario, one of the best players in the world on clay.

Serena was still learning to play on that surface, which makes the ball move slower and bounce higher than it does on hard surfaces. Still, early on she appeared to have the match under control, displaying a breathtaking variety of shot-making skills. When she needed to slam a backhand winner, she did so with ease. When she needed to make a more delicate shot, like a lob or a drop, she quickly adjusted. Sánchez-Vicario was off balance.

Then, late in the first set, Serena hit a return that Sánchez-Vicario argued had bounced twice before she hit it, an infraction of the rules. As Sánchez-Vicario pled her case to the referee, Serena approached the net, and the two got into an argument. The referee hadn't seen the double bounce and refused to change the call in Sánchez-Vicario's favor. On the next point, Serena won the first set, 6–4. Sánchez-Vicario slammed her racket to the ground in anger.

She turned that anger into powerful play and took the second set, 7–5.

In the third set, Serena was losing when she inadvertently struck a shot that nearly hit her opponent.

Sánchez-Vicario took offense. After winning the match with a third-set score of 6–3, she let everyone know how she felt about Serena.

"She doesn't have respect for the other person who is across the net," the Spanish-born player told reporters. "So I win the match and I show her. I teach her a lesson."

Serena was accustomed to opponents questioning her aggressive style of play and competitiveness. She didn't apologize for playing hard. "Everything is a learning experience for me," she said.

She had another learning experience a month later at Wimbledon. Midway through the first set of her third match, she slipped on Wimbledon's grassy court and injured her left calf. She tried to play through the pain, but couldn't. She was forced to default, giving the win to her opponent, Virginia Ruano Pascual.

"I could have carried on if I wanted to," Serena told reporters later, "but I have to think about the future. I don't want to hurt myself over something silly and be out for two months just because I didn't stop."

Venus, meanwhile, was still very much in the tournament. When asked about her sister's chances, Serena gave a lighthearted reply. "She might go a long way now that I'm out of the draw. I'll give her a couple of tips."

Venus went as far as the quarterfinals that year before losing a contentious match that saw her loudly protesting, even crying, over what she thought were bad line calls.

With their Wimbledon hopes dashed, Serena and Venus set their sights on the US Open. Venus reached the semifinals but lost to the eventual winner, Lindsay Davenport. Serena, meanwhile, only lasted to the third round, when Irina Spîrlea took her revenge and defeated her in three sets. There would be no Grand Slam title for either Williams that year.

Yet there was no denying that the Williams sisters were on the rise. Venus ended the year ranked sixth, and Serena, after only one full season of tournament play, was ranked twentieth.

Women's tennis would never be the same again.

✶ CHAPTER TEN ✶

1999

Growing Stronger

Serena's first full year as a professional tennis player had been a strong one. The losses to Venus had been hard on her, though. For Venus's part, defeating her younger sister held little joy for her. It was also hard on their parents. So the family made a decision that the girls would play separate schedules as much as possible in the coming season.

Being apart was challenging for Serena and Venus. They weren't just sisters; they were best friends. Their close-knit relationship had only grown stronger in recent years, in part because they'd had trouble making new friendships with other players.

There were many reasons for that difficulty. One was that the other players had known one another for years because they had played together as juniors. Venus and Serena were newcomers who didn't always reach out to the other women. The attention Venus and Serena received was another hindrance to new friendships. It wasn't their fault that reporters and fans sought them out, but it rankled more experienced, accomplished players, who sometimes felt they were more deserving of the limelight. It didn't help that the confident Williams sisters didn't always act with the deference that many people in tennis expected. This attitude irritated some observers and players.

Finally, others were put off by the success of two black women in a predominantly white sport. Richard Williams, whose outspokenness on a variety of issues hadn't made him very popular with the tennis establishment to begin with, frequently brought up the significance of his daughters' race—even though some people didn't want to hear about it.

Serena didn't talk much about the backlash against her family. Instead, she chose to let her prowess on the court speak for her.

And speak it did, loud and clear. After competing in the 1999 Australian Open, where she lost in the third round, she played her way to the finals of the Open Gaz de France in Paris. There she faced Amélie Mauresmo. She was still looking for her first tournament victory. After winning the first set, 6–2, she lost the second, 3–6. It all came down to the final set.

Serena jumped ahead 4–1, but Mauresmo fought back to make it close. The match went to a tiebreaker. Serena fired an ace to take control and went on to win it 7–4 and the set 7–6.

"I have always dreamed of winning Grand Slams and this is a start," a jubilant Serena said later. "It's good to win a smaller tournament because when I get to the big events I will have the experience." It was also good to win the $80,000 that came with the victory. She immediately sent her sister an e-mail to give her the good news.

Half a world away in Oklahoma, Venus was competing in the IGA SuperThrift Tennis Classic. "I found out she won before I came out to play my match," she said. "I really felt it was my duty to come out here and win."

She got right to work versus Amanda Coetzer. In a stunning performance, she dispatched her opponent in only fifty-eight minutes, winning 6–4, 6–0.

Richard Williams, who accompanied Venus to Oklahoma while Oracene went with Serena to France, was ecstatic. "It makes me think about where we came from, out of the ghetto. To have them both win...brought tears to my eyes."

Now that Serena had broken through with a win, she was eager for more. It didn't take her very long.

One week later at Indian Wells, California, Serena dominated the field, beating every opponent, including the heavily favored Lindsay Davenport, to reach the finals. There she faced very stiff competition in the form of superstar and fan favorite Steffi Graf. Graf entered the tournament with 106 titles. She had beaten Serena earlier that year at a tournament in Sydney, Australia.

Graf would not add number 107 in California, however. Serena powered past her to take the first set 6–3, then rebounded after a second-set 3–6 loss to go up in the all-important third set 6–5.

To win the match, Serena needed to break Graf's serve. The championship point was a baseline duel between the two heavy hitters. Serena's effort could be heard in the loud grunts that accompanied every stroke. Then it happened — Graf hit a forehand that sailed out.

The crowd erupted with cheers. Serena leaped for joy and raced to the net to kiss Graf on both cheeks before jumping and laughing some more. "This win means a lot to me because Steffi is a great champion," Williams told reporters afterward. "I had a tough match with her earlier this year in Sydney and I knew it would be tough today too. This is the biggest tournament I've ever won. I know that I can win the big ones now."

Serena, who won $215,000 that day, acknowledged that it helped her knowing she wouldn't have to face her sister. But it was impossible for the sisters to avoid each other entirely—as they soon found out.

★ CHAPTER ELEVEN ★

1999

Almost...

The Williams sisters stayed out of each other's way at the start of the 1999 tournament schedule. But they both decided to play in the lucrative Lipton Championships at the end of March. When the draw came out, the girls immediately realized that if they each won the matches in their draw, both would reach the finals and face each other.

This time, Serena looked forward to that possibility. She had grown and matured, and after her win at Indian Wells, was feeling confident. She made it to the Lipton semifinals without really being tested. But tennis fans wondered if she'd have trouble with her opponent, Martina Hingis. She did, but in the end, defeated her 6–4, 7–6 to reach the finals.

Venus, meanwhile, played her way to the championship round, too, beating Steffi Graf in the semis 6–2, 6–4. It was to be a Williams-Williams final!

A sister showdown hadn't occurred in the finals of a major tournament since Maud and Lillian Watson played each other at Wimbledon in 1884. All of a sudden, everyone seemed to recognize that the Williams sisters were as good as their father had been predicting they would be.

Both seemed to look forward to the matchup. "I've always been in the background," said Serena. "It's time for me to move forward."

Venus wasn't so sure about that. "I don't like putting my name and losing in the same sentence," she said. "Winning and Venus sounds great."

When Venus and Serena took the court for the final, the atmosphere was electric. The old hit song "We Are Family" by Sister Sledge blared over the loudspeakers. The crowd was unlike any other ever seen at a WTA final. People of all ages and colors packed the stands to witness history. Richard Williams was unable to contain his pride as he paraded through the stands with a sign that said WELCOME TO THE WILLIAMS SHOW.

That's exactly what it was. The match was one of the most anticipated in the world of tennis, and millions watched on television.

But the sisters found that playing each other caused some special problems, just like in their match at the

1998 Australian Open. Nerves seemed to get the better of them.

Serena had been playing great tennis, winning sixteen matches in a row, and was favored by many to win. But in the opening set, she had a hard time getting her head in the game. Venus didn't play very well, either, but still managed to win, 6–1. Both sisters settled down in the second set. Serena fought hard and won, 6–4. The match would be decided in the final set.

That's when the sisters started playing the kind of tennis that spectators had turned out to see.

Down 2–4 in the final set, Serena suddenly rallied. In the seventh game of the set, she demonstrated just how badly she wanted to win.

In the midst of one long rally, she hit a forehand out-of-bounds. She reacted by throwing her racket toward her courtside chair. It bounced wildly and struck a television cameraman, earning her a warning.

A few minutes later, in another long rally, Venus charged the net. Serena came back with a hard forehand smash.

Thwack! The ball struck Venus on the wrist. Both sisters were playing as hard as they could.

Serena fought back to tie the set at 4–4, but the

effort seemed to exhaust her. She lost eight of the next nine points to lose the set 4–6, and the match. Venus was the Lipton champion.

She didn't celebrate her win, though. Expressionless, she simply walked to the net, slapped hands softly with her sister, then put her arms around her. The two walked off the court together.

Venus's victory was bittersweet. She knew that her sister felt bad about losing to her again. But Serena refused to let her disappointment rule the day. "We believe that family comes first, not a game," she said. "Why would I want that to come between someone who has always been around, always been a very special friend for me? I couldn't imagine that and I don't think she could either."

Still, Serena wasn't ready to give up. "I definitely look forward to another final with Venus. It's what we always dreamed of," she said. "Now that my game is taken to a different level, it's going to happen more."

There was one thing in particular Serena had always dreamed of—a Grand Slam win. Whether she could turn the dream into a reality, however, remained to be seen.

★ CHAPTER TWELVE ★

1999

Stoked

After the Lipton Championships, both Serena and Venus set their sights on the 1999 French Open, Wimbledon, and US Open. Most observers expected one of the sisters, if not both, to win her first Grand Slam event. Perhaps they'd even face each other in one of the finals.

It didn't happen at the French Open. Serena lost in the third round, and Venus was booted in the fourth.

Next up was Wimbledon. As the sisters prepared for the lush grass surface, the draw was announced. If Serena and Venus each made it through the first three rounds, they would face each other in round four. But when the sisters arrived in England, nothing went as planned.

Just before the beginning of the tournament, Serena contracted the flu and was forced to withdraw. There would be no Williams-Williams showdown on center court.

Serena's withdrawal appeared to open the door for Venus. Her path to the finals suddenly seemed a lot easier.

But it was not to be. Venus, too, came down with a touch of the flu. Although she fought through the illness and made it to the quarterfinals against Steffi Graf, she went no further. The three-set classic, which took an amazing seven hours to complete because of long points and longer rain delays, ended with a disappointing 2–6, 6–3, 4–6 loss for Venus.

The sisters began to look ahead to the US Open in early September. It would be the last time the two would play in the same tournament in 1999 and the last chance either would have to win a Grand Slam title that year.

The tennis facility at Flushing Meadows, New York, had recently been rebuilt and renamed after Arthur Ashe, the trailblazing African American men's champion, who had passed away several years before. There was no better place in the world for a Williams to win.

When the draw for the Open was announced, Venus was seeded number three and Serena number seven. They were in different brackets, and that set up the possibility of another all-Williams final. "I hope we can do that well," said Venus. "It would be great."

Both sisters made it to the semifinals easily. The champion of the tournament would come from among the remaining four players — Serena, Venus, Lindsay Davenport, and Martina Hingis.

In the minds of many, those four were the best women's tennis players in the world. Each exhibited a slightly different style of play. Venus was all power and speed. Davenport could easily match her power. Serena had the skills and shot-making ability to play both a power game and a baseline game, while the savvy Hingis was best known for her consistency and finesse. No matter who ended up in the final, a great tennis match seemed certain.

Serena faced Davenport in the first semifinal. In order to win, she knew she'd have to keep her opponent on the move and wear her out. If she allowed Davenport to set up her powerful returns, Serena could be in trouble.

Serena worked her game plan to perfection in the first set and won, 6–4. She was one set away from reaching the finals.

But in the second set, she fell behind, then fell apart. Shots she had made with ease in the first set suddenly went awry. Davenport stormed back to defeat her, 6–1. With only one set remaining, Serena had to scramble to come up with a solution.

She found her answer in her serve. She started the match by serving three rockets for aces, stopping Davenport in her tracks. Now she had a chance.

The two players fought it out for the remainder of the set, but in the end Serena came out on top, winning 6–4 to take the match and earn a place in the finals. "I just stayed determined and focused," she said later.

As the two left the court, Venus and Hingis took over and began to practice. Serena showered, then rushed back to cheer her sister on.

Venus needed the support. Hingis ran her all over the court and eventually came away with a 6–1 win in the first set. Those games were actually much closer than the final score indicated, however, and that seemed to give Venus hope. Known for her stamina, she made Hingis work for every point in the second set. In the end, Venus won, 6–4.

But her comeback came with a cost. The weather that September afternoon was hot, and Venus became dehydrated. Dehydration led to cramps. That was the only advantage Hingis needed. As she said later, "I tried to keep her running. I knew she was cramping."

Hingis drew away in the middle of the set, and Venus was powerless to keep up. She lost, 3–6. There would be no all-Williams final.

Serena felt terrible for Venus, and Venus was certainly disappointed. But there was a silver lining. Her tough match with Hingis may have helped tire out her sister's opponent. "Now [Serena's] playing for two people. Hopefully, I gave Martina a good workout today."

When the two young women took the court the next day, it soon became clear that Hingis was indeed tired. In contrast, Serena looked quick and strong.

In the first set, Serena overwhelmed her opponent, running her all over the court and reaching every return Hingis made. She cruised to a 6–3 first-set win.

But Hingis, despite being only eighteen years old, was a veteran of many tennis wars. She sensed that her own game was off, abandoned her usual attacking strategy, and instead just kept the ball in play, hoping Serena would make some mistakes.

The new strategy worked. In the second set, Serena

began to tire and made some unforced errors. Hingis believed that if she could just get the match to a third set, she'd outlast her opponent.

Nevertheless, Serena took a 5–3 lead. She needed only one more game to win the tournament.

But Hingis didn't give in. She stuck to her plan and hoped that Serena would be too anxious to win.

The two battled to match point, but Hingis fought Serena off to take the game and make it 5–4. Then Serena took her to match point a second time. Once more, Hingis calmly fought her off to eventually tie it 6–6. The match would go to a tiebreaker.

The pressure was on Serena. If she lost, she was almost certain to suffer a letdown in the third set. Hingis would have a good chance to come back and win.

Serena didn't want the match to go to a third set. She wanted to win now.

Drawing on inner resolve and physical strength, she used her serve and a series of powerful ground strokes to inch ahead. With the score 6–4 in the tie-breaker, she stood getting ready to serve, knowing that if she won this point, the US Open championship — a Grand Slam title — would be hers.

She took a quick glance toward the stands and

drew a deep breath. It was as if her entire tennis career had come down to one shot. Thousands of hours of practice were distilled into a single moment.

She bounced the ball on the ground several times, then held it before her in her left hand, her racket in her right hand hanging at her side. The stands were absolutely quiet. She tossed the ball into the air and exploded, hoping for an ace.

Thwack! The serve boomed across the net, nicking the inside corner of the service box.

Hingis reacted quickly and connected. Serena returned it with a powerful backhand. Hingis swatted it back. Serena fired off another backhand to Hingis's backhand. Hingis got to the ball, swung, and hit it. The ball soared over the net, heading for the baseline. Serena was on her toes, ready to pounce.

She didn't have to. Unbelievably, the ball soared out! Serena had won the US Open, her first Grand Slam title!

Her knees buckled and she staggered backward, a look of utter surprise and amazement on her face as the crowd erupted in cheers. She held her quivering hands to her face and began screaming, "Oh my God! Oh my God!" She looked around the stadium in disbelief as everyone stood and applauded.

In a daze, she congratulated Hingis and stepped to one side of the court for the trophy presentation, basking in the applause as an engraver quickly added the name Serena Williams to the illustrious list of former champions, which included Althea Gibson, Chris Evert, and Martina Navratilova. When she received the trophy, she looked at it closely. "There's my name right there," she said, drawing her finger across the line.

A few moments later, a tennis official handed her a phone. President Clinton was calling to offer his congratulations. Serena was in a daze. When he asked her how she felt, she blurted out, "I'm pretty stoked!"

So was the rest of the tennis world.

★ CHAPTER THIRTEEN ★

1999–2000

Golden Girls

Serena was on a roll. Just a month after winning the US Open, she defeated Venus for the first time, beating her in three sets to win a title in Munich, Germany. "I was cruising today," she said afterward. "I'd never actually beaten Venus; I didn't know how it feels."

Venus did. Although she tried to put her defeat into perspective, saying, "It's a win-win situation. One daughter is going to win. What's the difference?" the loss served as a wake-up call. As much as the sisters tried to deflect attention from their emerging rivalry, neither young woman liked to lose.

Venus hoped to capture her first Grand Slam title in 2000. She knew that until she did that, she would never be considered a truly great player.

Serena and Venus got off to slow starts in 2000, as each was hampered by tendonitis of the knee. For a while, there were even rumors that Venus would retire. But as spring turned to summer, both sisters recovered and began to play better tennis. Because of the injuries, they had missed out on chances to win a Grand Slam title at the Australian and French Opens. Both looked forward to Wimbledon in July, hoping to capture that elusive championship.

To no one's surprise, they both reached the semifinals. To their dismay, they would play each other.

Their match was one of the most anticipated events in Wimbledon history. But once again, the matchup was a critical disappointment. With so much at stake, the sisters seemed to have a hard time playing very well against each other. Richard Williams couldn't even bear to watch. He walked the streets around the All England Club while his two daughters battled it out.

Serena was off her game from the very beginning. Venus played steady if unspectacular tennis and won the first set easily, 6–2.

Serena fought back in the second set, which went to a tiebreaker. Then her serve deserted her. On match point she double-faulted. As her final serve plunked into the net, she blinked back tears. Venus walked over to her, put her arm around her, and slowly escorted her off the court.

Serena was crushed, not so much because she lost to her sister, but because she knew she hadn't played very well. "I expected to play a lot better," she said, barely holding back tears. "It was my goal to do better."

Venus seemed to take little joy from the win. "It's not really so much fun. If it was a final it would have been different, but it was a semifinal and I hated to see Serena go."

This time, it was Serena's turn to sit in the stands during a Grand Slam final and cheer for her sister to win — which is exactly what Venus did, beating Lindsay Davenport in straight sets, 6–3, 7–6, to claim her first Grand Slam victory.

After the win, Venus raced over to give Serena a hug. Serena started crying, this time with tears of joy.

Tennis fans could hardly wait for the US Open in September. It seemed almost certain that the Williams sisters would meet in the finals. Serena would be looking to defend her title, and Venus would be hoping to win a second consecutive Grand Slam. In recent months, the sisters had been almost unbeatable.

But Serena received a tough draw in the tournament. She faced Lindsay Davenport in the quarterfinals and was eliminated.

That opened the door for Venus. But even as she readied herself, a shadow fell over the tournament. Reports that Davenport and Hingis had made a promise to each other to do whatever they could to prevent an all-Williams final started to circulate. When asked, Davenport admitted that it was true. "Martina and I had a little talk...we didn't want that to happen."

Some observers criticized Davenport for her remarks. After all, the US Open was an American tournament. It didn't seem right for her to root against another American.

Although the Williams sisters were much more popular with other tour members than they had once been, there was still some resentment over their success and unorthodox style. Rumors had circulated for years that Richard Williams decided which daughter would win when the two faced each other, and that they sometimes worked as a team in tournaments, extending matches to wear down certain opponents for the benefit of the other.

The sisters dismissed such reports as sour grapes. Rather than extend the talk in the papers, Venus let her play speak for her. And it spoke very loudly in the semifinals, where she beat Hingis in a tough three-set match, and again in the finals, where she dispatched Davenport after nearly two hours of play to come away with her second consecutive Grand Slam win.

She and Serena had little time to celebrate, however. Just a few weeks later, they traveled to Sydney, Australia, for the 2000 Olympics. Venus had been named a member of the American women's team, one of two players, along with Davenport, competing in singles. Serena made the team as well, paired with Venus in the doubles competition.

They had partnered many times before and in fact had won twenty-two consecutive doubles matches in tournament play. They looked forward to playing side by side on the world tennis stage.

Serena and Venus also looked forward to working with US team coach and world-renowned player Billie Jean King and her assistant, former champion Zina Garrison. King and Garrison worked them hard, impressing upon the sisters the necessity of teamwork. Even though they were on a big winning streak, they tended to overpower their opponents with their individual skill. King and Garrison wanted them to learn to work together more.

The young women took that lesson to heart. In one of the most dominating performances in Olympic history, they crushed the opposition, losing only one set on their way to the finals. The only thing that stood in the way of a gold medal was the Dutch team of Kristie Boogert and Miriam Oremans.

All the years of practice, from the public courts of Compton to center court at the Grand Slams, came together for the sisters. They obliterated the two Dutch women, 6–1, 6–1, to take home the gold for the United States.

From the looks of things, there would be many more golden moments in their future. But one question continued to dog them: would one Williams eventually prove to be stronger?

★ CHAPTER FOURTEEN ★

2001

Indian Wells

Serena Williams has played in hundreds of tournaments over the course of her career. Win or lose, most of those tournaments were positive experiences. A few, however, were not.

One of those was the 2001 Indian Wells tournament. Serena had won her second ever WTA victory there in 1999. While she hadn't defended it in 2000, she returned to the California courts at the top of her game and eager to reclaim the title. Venus was there, too, and looking to post a win herself.

With familiar names on the schedule—Hingis, Davenport, Seles—and strong newcomers in the mix, Serena and Venus expected to face tough competition, including each other. What they didn't expect was an enormous controversy. But that's just what they got.

Indian Wells takes place in a hot, dry desert area of

California. Faced with these conditions, athletes need to be sure to stay well hydrated. Unfortunately, in her quarterfinal match against Elena Dementieva, Venus neglected to do just that. She cramped up and then, to make matters worse, injured her knee. Somehow, she managed to pull off a win, but she was hurting.

Serena also won her quarterfinal match. The sisters would once again battle in the semifinals.

Except they didn't. On the day of the match, Venus was still hurting. Rather than risk worsening her injury, she told Serena she was going to withdraw.

Tournament protocol required Venus to get the athletic trainer's approval before withdrawing. The trainer was then supposed to inform the tournament director, who would have the unpleasant task of announcing to spectators that one of the star players would be dropping out. Obviously, this would not make the spectators happy. They had paid a lot of money to see the premier players in action.

That may be why the trainer and director delayed the announcement until the last possible minute. The fans were already in the stands when they heard the news. Not surprisingly, they were outraged. But they weren't mad at the officials. They were mad at Venus, Serena, and Richard.

There had been rumors circulating for a few years that Richard "fixed" his daughters' matches; that is, he told one of them to let the other win. Like so many other rumors, this one had no basis in fact, but it spread like wildfire throughout the tennis world. At Indian Wells, the wildfire flamed out of control, although the Williamses didn't know it until the finals.

With Venus's withdrawal, Serena automatically advanced to the championship round against Kim Clijsters. Serena and Clijsters had met twice before, once at the 1999 US Open and once the year before at Indian Wells. Serena had won both times, so when she walked onto the court for her warm-ups, she felt confident about her chances.

Then she heard the crowd booing.

"They were loud, mean, aggressive...pissed!" she recalled. "The ugliness was just raining down on me, hard."

The ugliness included racial slurs and demands that she go back to Compton. Serena hoped the shouts would cease when the match started. But they just got louder. She waited for the officials to control the crowd. They didn't. She looked to Clijsters to say something. Clijsters didn't, though Serena believed that she, too, was being affected by the yells, even though they weren't directed at her. Every now and then, someone would call out something positive to Serena, but those calls were few and far between.

In the face of such ugliness, Serena did what her father had taught her all those years ago. She channeled her emotions into her play. After losing the first set 4–6, she wore Clijsters down to win the second 6–4 and the third 6–2.

Serena drew on her strong religious faith when the match ended and gave a short, gracious interview from the court. "I'd like to thank everyone who supported me," she said, her voice cracking with emotion, "and if you didn't, I love you guys anyway."

Indian Wells left a profoundly negative impression on Serena. She would later tell interviewers that she cried the whole way home even though she was holding a trophy. She vowed to stay away from the venue, saying, "Indian Wells clearly didn't need me, and I didn't need that."

Serena pushed Indian Wells from her mind. She would soon face a bigger, more important challenge: recapturing her US Open title from the reigning champion — Venus.

★ CHAPTER FIFTEEN ★

2001–2002

Sister Slam

The 2001 US Open had many firsts. It was the first time a women's major sporting event was shown on television during prime-time hours. It was the first time two African American women competed for the title. And it was the first time the Williams sisters would face off for the US championship.

The tennis world was in a frenzy of excitement. The sisters were two of the most dynamic players in the sport. They'd been playing well in the tournament, besting top opposition with an impressive combination of power and finesse. People were anticipating an electrifying match.

Venus, ranked fourth in the WTA, went into the match with a record of forty-five wins and only five losses, and a whopping $1,661,610 in prize money for 2001. Serena was ranked tenth. Her record stood at thirty-five wins and six losses, with $900,263 in prize money. Neither was thinking about rank, win/loss records, or money when they took their positions at center court in Arthur Ashe Stadium, of course. Each was thinking about what it would take to beat her opponent.

Serena served the first game and won. Up 30–0 in the second, she was making Venus run corner to corner when she dumped back-to-back forehands into the net to tie it up at 30–30. The sisters each earned another point to tie it at deuce. To win the game, one of them had to get two points in a row. That didn't happen for a few minutes, for they traded points to return the score to deuce. Finally, Serena hit two returns out to give Venus the game.

Serena took the third game thanks to a powerful ace that clocked in at 119 miles per hour and a passing shot that ripped right by her sister. But Venus stole the set from her by winning the next five games in a row.

In the second set, the women battled to an even 4–4. Then Serena seemed to lose her edge. She double-faulted twice in a row to go down 0–30, then hit a shot that went just wide. She got a point when Venus dumped the ball into the net, but lost the game when Venus drilled an unreturnable ball just beyond her reach.

Serena was down but not defeated. On Venus's first serve, Serena blasted a return that touched down deep in the forehand corner, where Venus couldn't hit it back. But then she committed an unforced error, hit a ball into the net, and sent another sailing out. Venus was just one point away from defending her US Open title.

Venus moved to the service line. The officials shushed the excited crowd. She took a deep breath, tossed the ball into the air, and unleashed a ferocious shot that clocked in at 121 miles per hour. It didn't go in, however.

The second serve did. The sisters battled back and forth for six shots. And then on the seventh, Serena whacked it into the net. With the misfire, her racket flew out of her hands and bounced across the court.

There would be no title for Serena. Venus had won.

The crowd went wild. The sisters didn't. Serena retrieved her racket and jogged to the net to embrace her sister. Neither woman was smiling.

Venus seemed subdued in the post-final interview. She knew Serena was hugely disappointed, and that made Venus feel terrible. "I always want Serena to win," she said with a gentle smile. "I'm the big sister. I take care of Serena."

Serena echoed her sister's affectionate words in her own interview, and then did her best to put a positive spin on things. "I'm still young, I'm only nineteen and I have a few more years out there."

Serena ended her 2001 season with a win in late October. It was an underwhelming victory, however, earned not by her play but because her opponent, Lindsay Davenport, was forced to withdraw with a knee injury.

A few months later, Serena herself bowed out of the semifinals of her first 2002 match, the Medibank International in Sydney, Australia, after spraining her right ankle while chasing after a drop shot hit by fellow American player Meghann Shaughnessey. The injury was still plaguing her a week later, sidelining her from the first Grand Slam of the season, the Australian Open.

"It's tough because as a competitor I've set my goals a bit higher this year," she told reporters after pulling out.

When Serena returned to the court at the end of February, her competitive spirit was burning brighter than ever. She blew through the competition in a WTA tournament in Scottsdale, Arizona, and defeated Jennifer Capriati, who had roared back into the limelight after several down years, in the finals. A month later, she made history by defeating the three top-ranked players in the world—Hingis, Venus, and number-one Capriati—in Miami. She suffered back-to-back losses in April and May, first in Charleston, South Carolina, and then in Berlin, before posting a win in Rome. Along the way, she replaced Hingis at the number-three slot and was breathing down the necks of top-ranked Capriati and second-slot-holder Venus.

When she traveled to Paris for the second Grand Slam tournament of the season, the French Open, she had one goal in mind: win.

★ CHAPTER SIXTEEN ★

2002–2003

The Serena Slam

Twenty-one. That's how many consecutive Grand Slam matches Serena Williams won in 2002.

She began her unprecedented run at the French Open, beating her first four opponents with relative ease. In the quarterfinals, she added a fifth match by trouncing Mary Pierce, a tough competitor who four years later would suffer a career-ending knee injury, 6–1, 6–1.

That brought up Capriati, who proved to be a much greater challenge. Serena lost the first set, 3–6, then allowed Capriati to erase her 5–2 lead in the second. With the set tied at 6–6 and all the momentum on Capriati's side, Serena dug deep and powered ahead to win 7–6. That seemed to take the wind out Capriati's sails. She lost the third set to Serena, 2–6.

Serena was in the finals, where she would face her greatest nemesis and her best friend: Venus. This would be their fourth on-court meeting at a Grand Slam event. The previous three matches had been tense and hard-fought, for both sisters wanted to win but didn't want the other to lose. Each time, Venus had wound up consoling Serena.

At first, it looked as if history was going to repeat itself when Venus pushed ahead in the first set, 5–3. But Serena refused to quit. She powered past her sister with seven unanswered games to win the first set 7–5. She added three more to take a comfortable 3–0 lead in the second. Then Venus proved she deserved her number-two rank, winning three games to Serena's one to make it 4–3. Those were the last games she won that match, however. Serena outplayed her in the next two. Final score: S. Williams, 7–5, 6–3.

"I am so happy to have won my second Grand Slam in three years," Serena said after the win. "But obviously I am also a little bit sad for my sister."

Next up: Wimbledon. Once more, Serena decimated the competition to reach the championship round. So did Venus. And once more, Serena overpowered her sister, 7–6, 6–3, for the win.

The victory fulfilled a lifelong dream of Serena's and a promise she had made to herself earlier in the season. "I told myself I didn't care what else happens this year, I want to win Wimbledon...I wanted to be a part of history."

The Williams sisters met at center court a third time for the finals of the US Open. Tennis followers, even other top-ranked players, were captivated by the thought of a third Williams-Williams final. "Most amazing thing in sports almost," Lindsay Davenport marveled. "Could you imagine [pro golfer] Tiger Woods challenging a sibling to go head to head for all the majors? And in an individual sport, no less. They don't have teammates to help them along."

Venus entered the tournament as the two-time defending champion. She wanted to make it three. Serena, meanwhile, was eager to reclaim the title she'd lost to her sister in 2000. She loved Venus, but she loved winning, too. As she told one reporter before the prime-time outing, "Until 8:30 p.m., we'll be friends. When the match is over, we'll be friends again."

Gasps of amazement from the more than twenty-three thousand spectators in the stands that night mingled with the on-court grunts of effort made by the Williams sisters. Venus served first and won. Serena made it 1–1 with an unreturnable overhead smash to Venus's forehand. Venus battled back to win the third game despite losing points to her sister's powerful ground strokes. Serena served up a center-line ace to start the next game and then watched the ball land out on a desperate hit by Venus to finish the game.

Serena continued to push. So did Venus. They tied it up at 4–4. Then Venus seemed to lose focus. On a critical game point, she double-faulted to give Serena the lead. A few points later, Serena smacked a blistering ace that earned her the first-set win.

She took the second set, too, although Venus gave her a run for her money, erasing a 4–1 lead to 4–3. That was all the older sister could muster, however. Final score: S. Williams, 6–4, 6–3. Serena was once more the US Open champ!

A head-to-head comparison of the match showed just how much better Serena had played. She had one double fault compared to Venus's ten. Venus made thirty-three unforced errors; Serena had only nineteen. Serena hit sixteen winners while Venus had thirteen. Venus was clearly upset with herself, admitting that she "did make a lot of errors" while praising her sister's strong play and victory.

Serena had now won three Grand Slams in a row, all of them at her older sister's expense. Unbelievably, the Williams sisters met yet again at the next Grand

Slam, the 2003 Australian Open. And yet again, Serena came out on top, 7–6, 3–6, 6–4.

Winning four consecutive Grand Slams is an amazing achievement—so amazing that the tennis press gave it its own name: the Serena Slam.

Serena looked forward to giving the press something else to write about at the 2003 French Open. And she did, although it wasn't the kind of coverage she had hoped for.

CHAPTER SEVENTEEN

2003–2004

Trouble and Tragedy

A lift of the hand. In tennis, that's the signal a player gives to the chair umpire to indicate she isn't ready to receive a serve. According to the rules, if the server is already in motion when her opponent's hand goes up, she is allowed to retake the serve. So when Justine Henin-Hardenne, Serena Williams's opponent in the 2003 French Open semifinals, rose from her crouch and lifted her hand just as Serena was firing off her first serve, Serena assumed she'd be able to take the serve again. The ball had gone into the net, after all, because Serena had been momentarily distracted.

There was just one problem: the chair umpire didn't see Henin-Hardenne's hand go up. He instructed Serena to take her second serve.

Serena blinked in disbelief. She looked at her opponent, expecting her to verify that she'd given the "not ready" signal. Henin-Hardenne didn't. Video later proved that Serena was in the right—Henin-Hardenne had definitely raised her hand. But at the time, Serena had no choice but to accept the chair umpire's ruling. Luckily, she made her second serve and won the point when Henin-Hardenne sent a forehand long.

The crowd at Roland-Garros responded by booing loudly and angrily. For some reason, they'd been against Serena all day, mocking her when she missed a return or flubbed a hit and cheering energetically for Henin-Hardenne when she earned a point. Serena had done her best to ignore their unsportsmanlike behavior, but the combination of the umpire's mistake, her opponent's refusal to admit having signaled, and the spectators' jeers finally broke her. She lost the next four points and, eventually, the match.

Serena was distraught afterward. "It was just a tough crowd out there today," she said through her tears, then added that she was disappointed with Henin-Hardenne. "To start lying and fabricating, it's not fair."

Serena put the loss behind her. A month later, she added another Wimbledon title to her list of achievements, beating—who else?—Venus. The win capped a stellar season marred only by the "hand incident," as the media was calling it. Wimbledon was also the last tournament she would play for more than eight months. Shortly after, Serena had surgery to repair a partially torn ligament around her left knee, an injury she sustained not on the tennis court, but while out dancing.

"Foolish" was how Serena described the injury later.

She kept busy during her recovery. In September, she traveled to Toronto to shoot a cable television show. While there, she received a strange phone call from her mother, who asked if she'd heard from her older sister Yetunde. Yetunde wasn't answering her phone, which concerned Oracene. Serena hadn't heard from Yetunde but assured her mother that everything was fine.

But everything was far from fine. On September 14, 2003, a gang member shot and killed Yetunde Price near Compton. The gang member meant to target her boyfriend, a member of a rival gang. But Yetunde became the victim.

Serena felt devastated. She and her sister Lyndrea were together when she got the news. "We were screaming and crying and consoling each other.... It was awful, just awful."

The man who pulled the trigger was caught and sentenced to fifteen years in jail. But his incarceration could not completely console the devastated Williams family. Tunde was gone.

Serena, Venus, and the rest of the Williams family mourned in private. Serena stayed away from tennis, using her knee injury as an excuse, though she later confessed, "I didn't think I was emotionally strong enough to start playing again."

Serena did eventually return, but her emotional state and the time away had taken their toll. Although she won her first title at the NASDAQ-100 Open in Key Biscayne, Florida, she lost in the quarterfinals of the 2004 French Open and suffered another crushing defeat in the finals at Wimbledon at the hands of up-and-comer Maria Sharapova. She fell out of the top ten rankings for the first time in years.

Then came the US Open. Her knee surgery had kept her from defending her 2002 title—Henin-Hardenne won the 2003 tournament—but she went into the event with some hope of recapturing the championship. She powered her way through the early rounds to reach the quarterfinals, where she faced Jennifer Capriati.

What happened during the hard-fought, deciding

set of that match left an indelible mark on tennis. Serena was serving. The game was at deuce when Serena sent a beautiful passing shot by Capriati. The ball kissed the court just inside the baseline to put Serena ahead.

At least, that was what Serena thought had happened. Umpire Mariana Alves, however, didn't see it that way. She called the ball out and gave the point to Capriati.

Serena couldn't believe it. "What happened?" she asked Alves, clearly stunned. "Excuse me? That ball was so in." In by at least six inches — she was sure of it. When Alves didn't reply, Serena headed toward her to contest the call.

At the time, tennis didn't have any way to confirm whether balls were in or out because the sport had no sideline instant-replay system. Television cameras caught every play, however, and showed questionable calls to viewers at home. Players, on the other hand, had to rely on line judges and chair umpires to make accurate calls. Understandably, mistakes were sometimes made; usually, the player who got the bad call just tried to move on.

That quarterfinal match had had more than its fair share of questionable calls, but this one was by far the worst. Few people needed a video replay to see that Serena's shot had been in. Commentators, people in the stands, and perhaps even Capriati knew it. Serena definitely knew it.

But Alves refused to overturn her call. Serena's lips tightened and she returned to the service line. She and Capriati battled to 5–4, Capriati with the one-game advantage and the serve.

Capriati lost the first point. Serena returned the next serve deep to the baseline.

"Out!" Alves cried.

Serena shot her a stare, then shook her head. Once more, she was certain the ball was in. Once more, video would prove her right. "Wow," one commentator said after watching the ball hit in slow motion. "Square on the line." Unfortunately for Serena, slow-motion instant-replay videos weren't available to umpires. The call, and the point, went to Capriati.

So did the next. And when Capriati won the point that followed, she won the quarterfinals, too.

Serena was furious. Even though she received an apology from tournament officials and had the satisfaction of learning that Alves had been banned from officiating any more matches that Open, the damage was done. She was out of the tournament.

There was one positive result from that day, however. The blown calls eventually led the tennis world to adopt Hawk-Eye, an instant-replay system that enables umpires to confirm calls—and correct bad ones, if necessary.

Years later, Serena admitted she should have tried to rise above the situation and keep her focus. But with her surgery and Tunde's death, her emotions were too raw to overcome. And unfortunately, her struggles weren't over.

★ CHAPTER EIGHTEEN ★

2004–2009

Ups and Downs

Serena finished off the 2004 season with a win at the inaugural China Open in late September and a loss in early November to Maria Sharapova at the WTA Tour Championships in Los Angeles. She repaid Sharapova by bouncing her from the semifinals at the 2005 Australian Open. It was a grueling two-and-a-half-hour match that left Serena worn out, and yet she went on to win that tournament, beating rival Lindsay Davenport, 2–6, 6–3, 6–0.

That was her only victory in 2005, however. In the months ahead, she failed to reach finals and often was eliminated in early rounds.

The 2006 season was even worse. She entered only four tournaments due to a knee injury. One of those was the Australian Open where she lost in the third round. "I cried," Serena later wrote. "Right there on the court... I still remember walking to the players' locker room after the match feeling so completely lost and beaten and confused." Her rank took a nose-dive, falling from seventh in 2004 to eleventh in 2005 and then plummeting to ninety-fifth in 2006.

People whispered that the once-unconquerable queen of the court no longer had what it took to be a champion. When the twenty-five-year-old entered the 2007 Australian Open ranked eighty-first and unseeded, those whispers grew louder. Detractors added that she looked out of shape.

But underestimating Serena Williams is never a good idea. The girl from Compton was strong, tough, and ready. Playing with a fury and impressive stamina, she pounded her way through the early rounds, winning three of her four matches in straight sets. She outlasted Shahar Pe'er in the quarterfinals, 3–6, 6–2, 8–6, to advance to the semifinals against Nicole Vaidisova. She dropped the Czech, 7–6, 6–4. One year after losing in the third round, Serena had reached the finals!

There she faced a familiar opponent, Maria Shara-pova. The nineteen-year-old Russian was riding a thirteen-match winning streak and looked poised to pick Serena apart.

Instead, Serena blew her off the court. Aces, over-head smashes, line-kissing backhands, and crazy spinning forehands—Serena dug deep into her arsenal of shots and came out firing from the first serve to the last. It took her just over an hour and a mere fifteen games to silence the whispers. Final score: 6–1, 6–2.

During the trophy ceremony, Serena's voice gave out as she made a short speech. "I would like to dedicate this win to my sister, who's not here.... I said a couple of days ago, if I win this it's going to be for her. So thanks, Tunde."

After the Australian Open, Serena set her eyes on the grand prize—or rather, the Grand Slam prize. She fit in a WTA tournament in Key Biscayne, battling back from a 0–6 first-set loss to beat the first-seeded Justine Henin (who had recently separated from her husband and dropped the last name Hardenne), 7–5, 6–3. Henin paid her back with interest, however, by trouncing Serena in the quarterfinals of the French Open, Wimbledon, and the US Open. There would be no Slam for the youngest Williams sister that year.

Or the year after. She fell in the quarterfinals at the Australian Open and was routed early on in the French Open. Then, in July, she roared back into the headlines by reaching the Wimbledon finals. So did another veteran of the All England Club grass courts, a twenty-eight-year-old who had battled injury and personal tragedy to emerge as the 2007 defending champion: Venus.

"This is what we've been aiming for," the older Williams sister told reporters during a joint interview.

"It's going to be a battle again. That's just how it is," Serena added.

The match took place on a windy Saturday in early July. It had been five years since the sisters had met on the center court green. As always, both came to win, but only one would emerge victorious.

Fans in the stands and watching at home were treated to an all-out Williams war, a slugfest featuring two of the strongest servers and fiercest competitors in the game. Venus and Serena played like strangers, often sending balls at each other's bodies. On one shot, Serena nearly drilled her sister in the face. Only Venus's lightning-quick reflexes saved her.

The score of the first set reached 4–4 then 5–4 before one sister pulled ahead. That sister was Venus. She won 7–5. The second set was the same 5–4 score in Venus's favor. She needed only one game to win.

She got it, although it wasn't easy. Serena rocketed a hundred-mile-per-hour ace past her on match point. That was her last point, however. She hit the next one wide. The match, and Serena's hope of winning that Grand Slam, was over.

She got the next one, though. After falling to Elena Dementieva at the summer Olympics in Beijing, Serena arrived at the US Open raring for a victory. She got it, beating Venus in a pounding quarterfinal match, then punishing Dinara Safina in the semis, and finally Jelena Jankovic in the finals.

"Watching her reminded me of a cross between a pit bull, a young Mike Tyson and an alligator," Richard Williams commented of his youngest daughter's ferocious play.

Dinara Safina was Serena's victim again in 2009, this time in the finals of the Australian Open. She failed to go further than the quarterfinals of the French Open, but played her way through to the championship match at Wimbledon, where she once more faced her sister. And this time, she won.

Everyone agreed: Serena was slamming again. But just a few short months later, it was Serena who was being slammed.

⋆ CHAPTER NINETEEN ⋆

2009–2011

Foot Problems

Serena was at the top of her game when she entered the 2009 US Open. She reached the semifinals, where she faced strong competition in Kim Clijsters. Clijsters had an answer for nearly everything Serena threw at her. Serena lost the first set 4–6. She was so angry with herself she slammed her racket to the ground, breaking it. The umpire called her for "aggravated behavior," a code violation that resulted in a warning. If she got another violation that match, she would forfeit a point to Clijsters.

The second set continued the battle. Serena was on the losing side, down 5–6. She fell behind in the next game, 15–30. Her first serve of the next point went wide. Her frustration showed in her expression and body language, but she tamped it down.

Until her second serve, that is.

Serena tossed the ball in the air just as she'd done

hundreds of thousands of times before. Knees bent, she whipped her racket up, around, and down, launching her body into the air and forward as the strings met the ball.

"Fault!"

Serena froze. Then she turned and looked at the lineswoman, Shino Tsurubuchi, in disbelief. Had she really just been called for a foot fault? She had!

The score changed from 15–30 to 15–40, advantage Clijsters.

Serena held herself together for a fraction of a second, accepting a ball for her next serve. Then suddenly, she snapped. Ball in hand, she advanced on Tsurubuchi, stabbing her finger, motioning with her racket, and yelling angrily.

Play halted. The chair umpire summoned the lineswoman over and asked what had happened. Tsurubuchi tipped her head back, pointed at her neck, and said Serena had just threatened to kill her by shoving the ball down her throat.

The lineswoman then returned to her seat. Moments later, Serena gestured and yelled at her again!

This time, the tournament director and another official headed onto the court. They called the lineswoman over. As they conferred, Serena joined them. They told Serena what Tsurubuchi had said.

Serena stared at the lineswoman, dumbfounded. "I didn't say I would kill you! Are you serious?"

In the end, it didn't matter what she'd said or didn't say. The officials slapped her with a second code violation for aggravated behavior. That infraction added a penalty point to Clijsters's side of the board. Because she'd only needed one point to win, the match was over!

Serena stormed to the other side of the court, tossing her racket as she passed the sidelines, and shook hands with a bewildered Clijsters. She left the stadium amid cheers and jeers. She learned afterward that she'd been fined $82,500 and put on probation for the next four Grand Slams. If she had another similar outburst, her fine would double and she would be banned from playing in the next US Open.

Serena later apologized for her outburst, admitting her behavior was "uncalled for" and "bratty." But she also voiced a strong opinion about the call that sparked it. "I don't think anyone should call a foot fault in the semifinals of a Grand Slam at that point," she said, "especially since I don't foot fault."

Serena put the controversy at the US Open behind her and focused on 2010. She began by defending her title at the Australian Open. That victory earned her the top place in the record books for the most wins at that tournament with five; only Margaret Court, Evonne Goolagong Cawley, Steffi Graf, and Monica Seles, who each won four, came close.

Soon after, however, she was sidelined with a leg injury. She played well when she returned in May, but not well enough to reach a final. Then came Wimbledon. Serena met with stiff competition on the grass courts, including Maria Sharapova, Petra Kvitova, and Vera Zvonareva. But she defeated them all in straight sets. It was her fourth Wimbledon and thirteenth Grand Slam since turning pro in 1995.

It was also her last tournament of the season.

In early July, Serena was leaving a restaurant in Munich, Germany, when she stepped on some shards of broken glass. At first she thought she'd just gotten a few minor cuts. Then she looked more closely.

"There was a massive puddle of blood," she told reporters later, "and I ended up fainting and needed stitches in both feet. I didn't know then but it was a torn ligament. I just know my toe was kind of hanging. They said it would be fine…but it ended up not being fine."

The slices and stitches took time to heal. And Serena's medical troubles were just beginning. On February 27, 2011, she was attending a party in Los Angeles to celebrate the Academy Awards. Suddenly, she started having trouble breathing. She tried to brush it off, but when it got worse, friends called for an ambulance. At the hospital, doctors told her she had a pulmonary embolism, or blood clot in her lungs. If they didn't operate immediately and remove it, she might die.

"I was on my deathbed at one point—quite literally," she later said.

They also discovered a hematoma, or buildup of blood beneath the skin, near her abdomen. This condition, too, needed treatment.

Fortunately, Serena was in superb health otherwise. She was cleared to return to the courts in early March. After almost a year away from the tournament scene, she wasn't in top form at first. But she slowly made headway, winning two minor events in the weeks leading up to the US Open.

And there in the finals at Flushing Meadows, trouble found her again. Or rather, she found trouble.

Serena's opponent was Samantha Stosur, an Australian who had suffered from a debilitating case of

Lyme disease a few years earlier. She'd made only four other Grand Slam appearances in her career. On paper, she seemed unlikely to beat Serena Williams. Yet that's just what she did in the first set, rolling over Serena, 6–2.

At the start of the second set, Serena was poised to chalk up a game for her side of the board. She hit a monstrous forehand. Certain it was a winner, she cried out an enthusiastic "Come on!" just as the ball cleared the net—and just as Stosur was reaching out to return the shot with a backhand. Stosur muffed the shot.

Yelling during someone's shot is an "intentional hindrance," a code violation. The chair umpire immediately enforced the rule, saying that Stosur's miss was a result of Serena's cry. She awarded the point to Stosur.

Serena had some choice words for the official during the changeover. After identifying her (incorrectly) as the same chair umpire who had "screwed her over" in the infamous Clijsters match in 2009, she warned the woman not to look at her if they ever encountered each other off the court. She accused the woman of being a "hater" and told her she was "unattractive inside."

Stosur went on to win the set—and the tournament. After her angry outburst and the loss, Serena looked strangely carefree during the trophy ceremony, smiling and joking with Stosur, who was later surprised when Serena pulled up a chair and sat down next to her.

"All of a sudden I turned around and she was right next to me, which is kind of unusual. She just said, 'How do you feel? Are you really excited? It's unbelievable.' It shows what a nice person she is and what a true champion she is; to be able to come over and congratulate your opponent I thought was pretty classy."

But not everyone in the tennis world agreed with Stosur. They believed that as a veteran of the sport and easily the most recognizable female player, she should have behaved better.

Serena, however, was unapologetic. To be fined for an inadvertent cry of triumph seemed wrong to her. She was a passionate player who put everything she had into every match.

If the tennis world had forgotten that, they were soon going to be reminded—big time.

☆ CHAPTER TWENTY ☆

2012–2015

Number One

The 2012 season began with a whimper for Serena, with a fourth-round elimination from the Australian Open. Soon after she suffered a staggering first-round defeat at the hands of Virginie Razzano at the French Open, her first such loss in ten years. Before and between these Grand Slam events, she was forced to withdraw from two tournaments due to nagging knee and back injuries. She lost two others and won only two.

But then something happened. Serena started winning. And winning. And winning.

Wimbledon in early July. The Bank of the West Classic in Stanford, California, in late July. Gold medals in both singles and doubles at the 2012 London Olympics in August. The US Open in September. And finally, the WTA Championships in October. Crisscrossing the globe, she played in fifty-eight events—and lost only four. Her Olympic victories earned her an elusive Career Golden Slam (all four Grand Slams and Olympic gold within a career) in both singles and doubles. She is the only player in tennis history to accomplish this amazing feat.

And she didn't stop there. In 2013, she won her first French Open since 2002. In September, she won her fifth US Open championship. But surprisingly, the highlight of her season came not after a win, but a loss.

That loss came in February at the Qatar Total Open in Doha, Qatar. Serena was disappointed—she hated losing—but even with the loss, she had amassed enough ranking points overall to bump up one notch on the WTA list.

How important was that bump? It moved her from number two—to number one! It was not the first time she had reached this pinnacle; that was back in 2002, when she was just twenty years old. But it was the hardest. Serena wasn't a youngster anymore, after all. In fact, at thirty-one years, four months, twenty-four days old, she jumped over Chris Evert to become the oldest woman to achieve the top rank. Her 2013 accomplishment was even more impressive considering that the year before her rank had dipped as low as 175th.

"I'm so sensitive nowadays, I'm always crying!" Williams said as she fought back tears. "I never thought

I would be here again. I've just been through so much and never thought I'd be here again."

Playing to the number-one rank is one thing. Staying at the number-one rank is something completely different. Everyone below you is fighting to take your place. At the start of the 2014 season, players were itching to oust Serena from her lofty spot.

For her part, Serena was looking to post a record-tying eighteen Grand Slam wins, a feat only tennis legends Martina Navratilova and Chris Evert had ever accomplished. It didn't come at the Australian Open, where she fell in the fourth round to Ana Ivanovic. She missed her chance at the French Open as well, where Garbiñe Muguruza dispatched her in the second round. Number eighteen eluded her at Wimbledon, too, when she fell to Alizé Cornet in the third round. If she didn't win the US Open, she'd have to wait until the next year to try for the record.

But win at Flushing Meadows was just what the two-time defending US Open champ did. She romped through the early rounds to reach the finals, where she faced her good friend Caroline Wozniacki. It took Serena just seventy-five minutes and eighteen games to send Wozniacki packing.

"It was an unbelievable moment for me," Serena

gushed afterward. "I've been practicing so hard and all that hard work was showing through today."

Not since Chris Evert in 1977 had a player won three US Opens in a row. Like Evert, Serena now owned six US Open championships in total. And of course, there was the other total she shared with Evert, and Navratilova, too: eighteen Grand Slam victories!

The hard work wasn't over. Serena continued to play tough and smart through the remaining events of 2014. And as it had in the US Open, her hard work paid off. She finished the season where she began — at number one.

Serena was strong in 2014. In 2015, she was virtually unstoppable. What did she do? Nothing but win the Australian Open, the French Open, and Wimbledon! Combined with her 2014 US Open championship, those three victories earned her a Serena Slam, her first since the 2002–2003 run from the French Open to the Australian Open. They also put her name in the record books as the first player since Steffi Graf in 1988 to win three Slams in a year. The Wimbledon win vaulted her over Navratilova as the oldest player to win that major. And those three Grand Slams increased her total to twenty-one, just one shy of Steffi Graf's long-standing record.

There was just one more Grand Slam for her to take: the US Open. If she won that, she'd add "calendar Grand Slam" to her long list of achievements. But first, she had to play her way to the finals.

She made it through the early rounds with relative ease. Then, in the quarterfinals, she faced one of her most challenging opponents, a player who had faded into the background a few years earlier only to resurge to greatness again. That player? Venus.

Once a dominant force on the court, Venus had suffered health problems in recent seasons. She revealed in 2011 that she had Sjogren's syndrome, an autoimmune disease that can cause muscle and joint pain and fatigue.

There is no cure, but Venus had learned to manage the symptoms of Sjogren's. She scaled back her schedule when necessary and withdrew from tournaments now and then. But nothing was going to keep her from meeting Serena at center court in Flushing Meadows.

And nothing was going to keep Serena from playing her sister as she would any other player—with all the power and finesse she could muster. Venus fought hard and took one set away from Serena, but in the end, she was no match for the younger Williams.

Serena won, 6–2, 1–6, 6–3, to advance to the semifinals and move one step closer to a calendar Grand Slam.

"She's the toughest player I've ever played in my life and the best person I know," an emotional Serena said of Venus after the match. "It's going against your best friend.... So it was really difficult today."

The next day was just as difficult. Serena faced Roberta Vinci of Italy—and lost. There would be no calendar Slam for her this year. After the loss, she received a special Twitter message from an admiring fan. "So proud of you, @SerenaWilliams," the tweet said. "What you did this year was amazing." It was signed "mo" for Michelle Obama, then First Lady of the United States.

Although she didn't say so, Michelle Obama may have been particularly proud of one other tournament Serena entered in 2015. After a fourteen-year boycott prompted by a barrage of hateful racial insults, Serena returned to Indian Wells. The crowd greeted her with cheers and massive applause, creating a welcoming environment that brought tears to Serena's eyes. While she had to bow out in the semifinals because of a knee injury, she was grateful to put the bad memories to bed at last.

★ CHAPTER TWENTY-ONE ★

2015 AND BEYOND

Onward and Upward

Serena finished 2015 still ranked number one. It was the fifth time she'd reached this goal and the third consecutive year. She held the rank until September 2016, tying her with Steffi Graf at 186 for the most consecutive weeks at the top. Then on September 12, Angelique Kerber, the newly crowned US Open champion, replaced her there.

Serena was disappointed, of course. To lift her spirits, she might have reflected on her year's highlights. At the top of the list was another victory at Wimbledon. It was her twenty-second Grand Slam title and the seventh time she'd won the All England Club classic. Only Martina Navratilova has more Wimbledon wins with nine. Serena went on to win the Australian Open in 2017, making her the only player—male or female—in the Open era to win twenty-three Grand Slam singles titles.

Or she might have taken stock of all she has accomplished, and continues to accomplish, off the court. For while Serena Williams is best known as a tennis player, she is personally involved in an amazing array of activities.

Nearest and dearest to her heart are the charitable organizations she supports. Through her fund, SW, she aims to provide help to "individuals or communities affected by senseless violence" and to ensure "equal access to education," according to her website, serenawilliams.com. Preventing gun violence, fighting for equal rights for women and minorities, offering scholarships to students who couldn't otherwise afford college, building schools in developing countries — these causes are Serena's passions.

So is fashion, an area in which she has shined for decades on and off the court. "I love things that an everyday woman can wear and still feel good and look good," she once said of her line of clothing and accessories. And she always turns heads when she debuts a stylish new tennis outfit at a tournament.

Serena has dabbled in the arts as well, providing voice-overs for cartoons and making appearances on a variety of television shows. She's written two autobiographies, *On the Line* and *My Life: Queen of the Court.*

Serena has been a hot topic in popular culture for years. She's been profiled in countless magazines, newspapers, and books; interviewed by famous personalities, such as Oprah Winfrey, and photographed hundreds of thousands of times; earned worldwide recognition as one of the most influential athletes in history.

How does she do it all? By staying positive and believing in herself. By setting her sights on her goals and working hard to achieve them. And most of all, by drawing on the love, support, and comfort of those who have stood by her side throughout every year of her life: her family.

Because in the end, as Serena once said, "Tennis is just a game. Family is forever."

Serena (right) and Venus (left) pose with their father, Richard, at the tennis courts in Compton, California.

Paul Harris/Online USA/Getty Images

Serena (right) and Venus (left) playing doubles at the 1999 TIG Tennis Classic in California.

Phil Anthony/Shutterstock

Sarah L. Voisin/*The Washington Post*/Getty Images

In 2001, Serena attends the opening of the Southeast Tennis and Learning Center in Washington, DC, and gives a new player a few pointers.

Ahead of the 2002 Winter Olympics in Salt Lake City, Utah, Serena joins in the torch relay.

Serena raises her trophy after winning the Australian Open singles final in 2005.

Serena chases down the ball to smash it back over the net.

lev radin/Shutterstock

Even when it looks like it would be a stretch, Serena's quick thinking and agility help her return the ball to her opponent.

At the 2013 US Open in New York, Serena captures her seventeenth Grand Slam singles title. She defeated Victória Fyódorovna Azárenka (left).

Serena on her way to a seventh Australian Open final in 2016.

Leonard Zhukovsky/Shutterstock

Career Highlights

(As of February 2017)

Rank: Tied the record for highest number of
  consecutive weeks at number 1 with 186;
  longest at number 1 (300 weeks total); oldest
  woman to achieve top rank
Win/Loss Record: 775–129
WTA Wins: 71
Grand Slam Tournament Wins: 23 (out of 29
  finals played)
  Australian Open: 7 (2003, 2005, 2007, 2009,
    2010, 2015, 2017)
  French Open: 3 (2002, 2013, 2015)
  Wimbledon: 7 (2002, 2003, 2009, 2010,
    2012, 2015, 2016)
  US Open: 6 (1999, 2002, 2008, 2012, 2013,
    2014)
Head-to-Head Record Versus Venus:
  Serena 17–Venus 11
Doubles Win/Loss Record: 184–30
WTA Women's Doubles Wins (with Venus): 23

Grand Slam Doubles Tournament Wins: 14
   Australian Open: 4 (2001, 2003, 2009, 2010)
   French Open: 2 (1999, 2010)
   Wimbledon: 6 (2000, 2002, 2008, 2009,
      2012, 2016)
   US Open: 2 (1999, 2009)
Total Mixed Doubles Grand Slam Wins (with
   Max Mirnyi): 2 (Wimbledon 1998, US Open
   1998)
Total Olympic Gold Medals: 4 (1 singles, 3
   doubles with Venus)
Total Tennis Prize Earnings: $84,428,451

Turn the page to discover another legendary female athlete's story

GREAT AMERICANS IN SPORTS

MIA HAMM

9

9

MATT CHRISTOPHER

INTRODUCTION

On the afternoon of August 1, 1996, more than seventy-six thousand spectators poured into Sanford Stadium on the campus of the University of Georgia in Athens, Georgia. There was nothing unusual about that. The university's football team, the Bulldogs, regularly packed the stadium with at least that many fans when they played their home games during football season.

The stadium wasn't packed with fans for a Georgia Bulldogs game or for any American football game, though. People from all over the world had come to Athens to watch a game of soccer. To be more specific, they had all come to see who would win the first gold-medal game in women's Olympic soccer, the United States or the People's Republic of China. Millions more across the world were watching on television as the superstar of women's soccer, Mia Hamm, led the United States against China's team. Never before had so many people gathered to watch a women's sporting event.

Only a few decades earlier, the idea that so many

people would watch a soccer game played by women would have been hard to believe. For most of the twentieth century, women were taken seriously in only a handful of sports. Track and field, golf, tennis, gymnastics, basketball, and figure skating were considered sports women could play without needing to be too physical. Many people thought sports like soccer were simply too rough for women to play. During those years, young women were constantly reminded of the notion that sports were for boys. Girls, on the other hand, were expected to engage in other activities—like homemaking, or standing on the sidelines and cheering on the boys. It wasn't until the introduction of Title IX, an amendment that outlawed gender discrimination at schools and colleges receiving money from the government, that women's athletics was finally given even a small portion of the attention it deserved.

Soccer, or what the rest of the world calls football, was the most popular sport in the world and started to become more popular in the United States as boys' and girls' youth leagues sprang up across the country during the late 1960s and early 1970s. But only a few women in the entire world played competitive professional-level soccer. Not many people even knew that women played soccer. In the United States, only a few high schools had a women's soccer team. It wasn't until 1978 that a college or university would field a varsity women's soccer program! There was no such thing as a national team or women's World Cup competition. No one thought that women would someday play soccer in the Olympics, let alone have their own professional leagues all over the world.

It was strong and talented women like Mia Hamm who changed all of that. Mia Hamm is without a doubt one of the greatest athletes of this century. Her playing and drive helped make the US women's national team one of the greatest in sports history. Mia caught the attention of the world with her play and became an ambassador for the sport. Her success has been hard-earned, and it all started when a toddler fell in love with soccer.

CHAPTER ONE
1972–1976

CHASING THE BALL

As the story goes, it was a warm day in 1973 when the toddler of the young Hamm family saw a boy and his father kicking a ball back and forth. No one in the family understood the game very well, but little Mia, the fourth of six Hamm children, loved what she saw. As she stood close to her parents, she never took her eyes off the black-and-white soccer ball. After a missed pass, she sprang after the ball and gave it one big whack. She had been born with a clubfoot, which required a corrective boot, and she was still learning to run and walk, but she managed to keep the ball from an older boy before giving the ball another mighty kick.

From that day forward, Mia dreamed of playing "the beautiful game," as soccer is often called. She didn't know that girls weren't "supposed to" play sports. For her, it was fun to chase after the ball and kick it, to run around with other children, then sit and play in the grass together, making friends.

That's how Mia Hamm's soccer career began. Years later, her love of the sport and the friendships she made on the field would take her all over the world and make her the most well-known female athlete of all time. But that was still a long ways off.

Mariel Margaret Hamm was born on March 17, 1972, in Selma, Alabama. Her father, William, was a pilot in the United States Air Force, and the family moved around a lot. Her mother, Stephanie, was a ballerina. Soon after she was born, her mother started calling her Mia because her daughter reminded her of one of her former ballet teachers, the world-famous ballerina Mia Slavenska.

As a member of the air force, Bill Hamm was never stationed in one place for very long. In 1973, he was transferred to Italy. The entire family, which then included Mia's older brother and two older sisters, moved to Florence, Italy.

When he wasn't flying airplanes, Bill Hamm loved to watch sports. But in Italy, hardly anyone played the sports Bill was used to watching in the United States. Bill liked baseball, football, and basketball. In Italy, the most popular sport was soccer, which was a huge part of the culture there. Men, women, and children all loved the sport. The stadiums on match days were always packed. The country would practically shut down when the national team played since everyone was focused on the game.

Wherever the family went, it seemed as if someone was playing soccer. In almost every open field or empty street, clusters of young boys raced after a soccer ball. Virtually every town had a men's team, and larger cities often supported several soccer clubs. Most teams were amateur, but the Italians also sponsored several thriving professional leagues. Thousands of fans turned out to support their favorite team, chanting and singing in unison in the stands while waving huge flags and banners. Televised soccer games were the most popular programs in the country.

When Bill started watching soccer, he didn't understand the game that well. Soccer wasn't very popular in the United States. Only a few public schools and colleges had soccer teams. The North American Soccer League was the professional league in America, but few people went to the games and they were rarely televised. Only a handful of the players were from the United States. Most were from Europe and South America. In the United States, Bill hadn't paid much attention to the game.

But in Italy, he had little choice. If he wanted to watch sports, he had to watch soccer. Luckily, soccer was everywhere. The more he watched, the more he began to appreciate the sport. He realized that what had first looked to him like a bunch of players randomly running after a ball was actually a sport that demanded great athletic skill and strategy. He learned that every player on the team played a specific position, just like in basketball or hockey, and each position had different responsibilities. The more Bill learned about the game, the more he grew to love it. It didn't take long for Italy to convert Bill into a rabid soccer supporter.

The family loved to do everything together, and Bill started taking his family to soccer games. The children, particularly Mia, took to the game immediately. She was small for her age and usually quite shy, but when she saw a soccer ball her eyes would light up. On the air force base, she often joined other children for pickup games of soccer.

When Bill was transferred to the United States a few years later, he and the Hamms brought soccer back with them. It had gotten under their skin. The only problem was that Bill and Stephanie would have to find soccer for their kids. Little League Baseball and other youth sports programs like Pop Warner football were commonplace in the United States, but youth soccer programs were still hard to find. When the Hamms finally landed in Wichita Falls, Texas, Stephanie and Bill were excited to find that youth soccer in Texas was as popular as football or baseball—or at least it was close.

Slowly but surely, soccer's popularity had risen in the States since the Hamms had moved to Italy. Brazilian soccer star Pelé, the best player to ever play the game, had signed with the New York Cosmos in 1975 and ignited an excitement for the sport in every major American city. The North American Soccer League (NASL) had gone from an afterthought to a real and viable league the moment Pelé signed with the Cosmos. His popularity and his play had started a soccer revolution in the United States. Teams had sprouted in Seattle, Los Angeles, Miami, Philadelphia, San Diego, and Portland, and even as far north as Vancouver, Canada. The NASL was growing at a phenomenal rate, and so was the popularity of the sport. Pelé's signing had opened the floodgates for soccer in America. Some of the best players from Europe began to pour into the US soccer market. European Footballer of the Year George Best; German World Cup winner Franz Beckenbauer; Bobby Moore, who captained England to the 1966 World Cup; three-time European Footballer of the Year Johan Cruyff; and Italian Giorgio Chinaglia all took a chance on the NASL in America. With the influx of talent, the games got more technical and more strategic, and the quality of the games improved dramatically. Americans were exposed to a level of soccer that had previously been seen only in Europe and South America—and they loved it.

The excitement of watching Pelé and the other great footballers of that era play the game as it was meant to be played had infected the country. Wanting to be just like their heroes, thousands of kids started joining youth leagues, and new leagues popped up in cities from coast to coast. Even after Pelé left the Cosmos and soccer's popularity dipped again in the United States, kids still had fun playing soccer, and adults were happy to organize teams and leagues. The game was so simple, and the fact that it didn't require a lot of equipment made it easy to start a new league in any state, and in most seasons. All it took was a grassy field and a ball, and players could learn the game. And anyone who could kick a ball or defend a goal could play. For parents, one of the best things about soccer was that every player got to touch the ball. Everyone was included.

Because soccer is a sport that relies more on speed and agility than strength and size, it is one of the few sports boys and girls can play together. Kids of similar ages, both male and female, are able to compete equally.

When Mia's older sisters and brother found out there was a league in town, they wanted to play. Bill was delighted and did his best to support his children. He was still learning the finer points of the game, so he started studying the rules and fundamentals of youth soccer. He became a coach and referee so that he could learn even more and make sure his children learned how to play correctly. He studied every book about soccer he could find.

At first, Mia wasn't allowed to play on a team. She was just too young. Yet the family spent most of every Saturday at the soccer field. Mia loved watching her siblings and the other kids play. Every time an errant kick came her way, she was off and

running after it. Her mother often spent her Satur-
days chasing after Mia!

Mia's mother recognized that her daughter was
full of energy, and thought she might enjoy taking
ballet lessons. Stephanie had loved ballet as a girl,
so maybe Mia would, too. Mia's mother enrolled her
in a dancing class.

"She was so petite, I thought she'd be ideal,"
Stephanie later said.

That's not quite the way it turned out. As far as
Mia was concerned, dance class was too slow. It
seemed that as soon as everyone in class started
moving, the teacher would stop the dancing so that
they could learn some other step. Besides, Mia
didn't like wearing ballet slippers.

As she told a reporter years later, "I hated it. I
lasted only one class."

Mia wanted to play soccer, just like the older
Hamm kids. Her mother understood. She remembered that when she was growing up, there weren't
many opportunities for girls to play sports. As she
later recalled, "Those of us who wanted to be active
found the joy in using our body in something like
dance. Now they have this other option and it's
beautiful." She put Mia's ballet shoes in a closet and

bought her a tiny pair of soccer cleats and a pair of shin guards.

Mia waited and waited and waited until she turned five, when she could join a team of her own. Finally, Mia would get her chance to show what she could do on the field. She was one of the smallest and youngest players on the team, but that didn't matter. Nothing could stop Mia once she started. She had grown up with the game, and playing all those years against her bigger, older siblings had made her tougher and stronger than the rest of the kids. She understood how the game was supposed to be played. She could see the game develop better than most and although she was timid at first, she quickly discovered that once she started scoring goals, she didn't feel so shy anymore.

As she remembered later, "Soccer was a way to hang out and make friends."

In time, it would become much more than that.

CHAPTER TWO
1977–1986

CHOOSING SOCCER

The opportunity to play organized soccer wasn't the only event of 1977 that had a big impact on Mia's life: Bill and Stephanie decided to add a new member to the family. Mia's parents adopted an eight-year-old Asian American boy named Garrett. Garrett was an orphan and the Hamms had love to spare. It was a perfect match.

Soon, Mia and Garrett were nearly inseparable. He, too, loved to play soccer and other sports.

"He was an instant playmate for me," Mia said. As Mia grew up, she tried to do everything Garrett did. "He let me hang out with him and his friends and play football, soccer, and basketball with them," she said.

Despite her small size, Mia was a good athlete. Garrett knew this, and called his little sister his "secret weapon" when the two would join his friends in the park for pickup games of baseball, football, basketball, and soccer.

"No one would want to pick me for their team," recalled Mia, "but Garrett would always pick me. We would downplay the fact that I was fast and could catch."

In the middle of the games, Garrett would give his secret weapon a look and Mia would start playing as hard as she could. One minute she was hanging back and the next she was running circles around the other children. She would get in behind the last defender to score the winning goal in soccer or catch the Hail Mary touchdown pass in football. Playing against the older kids helped Mia improve her skills faster than other children her age. Soon she wasn't a secret weapon anymore. It didn't take long for everyone to figure out exactly how talented she was and learn to watch out for her.

LITTLE, BROWN AND COMPANY
BOOKS FOR YOUNG READERS

Discover more at lb-kids.com

by MATT CHRISTOPHER.

Read all about Carter's and Liam's journeys in the Little League series

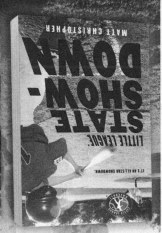

TWO PLAYERS,
ONE DREAM...
to win the Little League Baseball® World Series